PERSONAL AFFAIRS

SPEND, SAVE & INVEST
WISELY IN THE 90s

HOW TO GET WHAT YOU WANT FROM YOUR BANK

DOUGLAS GOOLD

MACFARLANE WALTER & ROSS
TORONTO

Macfarlane Walter & Ross
37A Hazelton Avenue
Toronto, Canada M5R 2E3

Canadian Cataloguing in Publication Data

Goold, Douglas, 1946–
    How to get what you want from your bank

Includes bibliographical references and index.
ISBN 0–921912–76–5

1. Banks and banking – Canada – Customer services.
2. Finance, Personal.   I. Title.

HG1616.C87G66 1994   332.1'7'0971   C94–932176–1

The publisher gratefully acknowledges the support of the Ontario Arts Council

Designed and typeset by James Ireland Design Inc.

Printed and bound in Canada

To Libby, with love

CONTENTS

ACKNOWLEDGEMENTS

I would like to thank those who so generously gave their time for interviews. While not all of them will agree with everything I say, I hope they feel that I represented their views fairly.

I took advantage of interviews I arranged for articles and columns I wrote in *The Globe and Mail* to ask Conrad Black, Bay Street veteran Andrew Sarlos and Tony Gage, president of Vancouver-based investment counsellor Phillips, Hager & North Ltd., for their views on the banks.

For the information and insights they gave me in interviews, I would like to thank them, as well as James R. Allen, Tom Alton, Lloyd Atkinson, Susan Bellan, Don Blenkarn, Laurie Campbell, K.J. (Ken) Cranston, Gerry Godsoe, Brien Gray, George Iny, John R. Kearns, Gerard Kennedy, Bob Kerton, J. David Livingston, T.F. (Tom) Mesman, Mostafa Moshtaghi, Dan Richards, Linda Routledge, Dr. Jim Savary, Pat Skene, Brian Smith, Larry Stevenson, Michael Stramaglia, C.M. (Duke) Stregger, A.S. Thompson, Paul Vessey, Peter Volpé, Kevin Wiltshire and Duff Young. Particularly helpful were Alan Silverstein, whose book, *The Perfect Mortgage,* was invaluable; Lawrence Brown, director, quality assurance, Equifax Canada; and Stephen W. Stewart, vice-president, personal lending, Toronto-Dominion Bank.

Peggy Wente, the editor of the *Globe*'s Report on Business, kindly agreed to allow me to take a leave of absence to complete the book. Robert Sutherland and Peter Goold provided me with valuable information.

Gary Ross proved to be a fine editor, and Wendy Thomas a careful copy editor. This book would not have been possible without the support and inspiration of Gary, Jan Walter and John Macfarlane.

I was fortunate to be able to persuade Sandra Martin, co-author of *Card Tricks: Bankers, Boomers and the Explosion of Plastic Credit,* colleagues Brian Milner and Bruce Little, Alan Silverstein, and Peter Volpé, vice-president of Integra Capital Management Corp. and past chairman of the Canadian Association of Financial Planners, to read parts or all of *How to Get What You Want From Your Bank.* Their suggestions have made it a better book, though they bear none of the responsibility for any errors or interpretations.

Finally, I would like to thank my wife Libby Znaimer, money specialist for Citytv, who read the entire manuscript, for her encouragement and support. I dedicate this book to her.

Douglas Goold
July 1994

I've been in banking 27 years,
and you can teach a monkey
any business after 27 years.
After all, it's not brain surgery.

MATTHEW BARRETT, CHAIRMAN, BANK OF MONTREAL

INTRODUCTION

More than 20 million Canadians deal with a bank, making it one of the most important and prevalent institutions in our lives. Yet there's precious little concrete information telling you how you can get a good deal when you walk into a branch to arrange for a credit card, loan, mortgage or new account, or to buy a mutual fund or GIC. *How to Get What You Want From Your Bank* will tell you how to get that deal, and how to save money.

If you're uninformed or intimidated, you won't make the savings that you could. And if you're having trouble with your bank, you'll be at its mercy unless you know what your options are.

I set out to reveal the real agenda of the banks – as opposed to what they say in their ads – and explain how they make decisions. How much does the bank need or want your business, and how much room do you have to negotiate or haggle?

This is a practical book, filled with tips on how to get the best deal, whether it's choosing the financing for your new car or a credit card that fits your spending patterns (it will also tell you how costly your credit card is, if you pay only the monthly minimum, and how the bank justifies interest rates of 15.75 per cent or higher). While there are no get-rich-quick schemes, I do describe a number of straightforward mortgage strategies, each of which can quite literally save you thousands of dollars. Most bankers don't have the time, knowledge or inclination to explain these to you.

1

You have to know them yourself – and take the initiative.

How to Get What You Want From Your Bank should help you untangle the 200 or so products each of the major banks now offers, a maze so complex that even bank staff have trouble finding their way through it. Which products make sense, and which are simply attempts by the banks' marketing departments to fill a perceived niche or to match the competition? It should also help you address some tough questions. Should you always be honest with your banker? Is doing so, if you are having financial problems, the equivalent of walking into the lion's jaws? What should you do if you are turned down for a credit card, a mortgage or a loan? What are your choices if you've never bothered to get credit in your own name but would like to establish some financial independence?

How to Get What You Want From Your Bank gets behind the banks' marketing hype. Are the banks really your "Small Business Partner," as they suggest? The sentiment is admirable, but in reality, the banks are interested only in low-risk lending. Their mantra is that they want to be right 99 out of 100 times. That explains why for years they have been at loggerheads with much of the small business community, which is willing to take risks.

The title of the book refers to "your bank," but might just as well have referred to "your financial institution." Because the major banks are so dominant in Canada, the focus is on them. But most of what's discussed also applies to the remnants of the trust industry and to credit unions and their Quebec equivalents, *caisses populaires.* Changes in legislation have greatly lessened the differences among these institutions, all of which offer broad ranges of products. In your search for financial products and services, you should include these institutions, as well as insurance companies, Treasury Branches in Alberta and Province of Ontario Savings Offices in Ontario.

I have been as specific and up-to-date as possible in my description of bank offerings. But since they change almost daily, readers are advised to check details with their financial institution.

Dominance of the Banks

Canada's big banks are among the largest in the world and dominate the financial services industry in Canada. They are poised to become even more dominant. With total assets (most of which are loans) of more than $660 billion, the six largest, from the biggest to the smallest, are the Royal Bank of Canada, the Canadian Imperial Bank of Commerce (CIBC), the Bank of Nova Scotia (Scotiabank), the Bank of Montreal, Toronto-Dominion (TD) and the National Bank of Canada, whose stronghold is Quebec. As Bay Street veteran Andrew Sarlos, known for his columns in the *Moneyletter*, told me, "Their power has become so great that in some respects it's frightening."

The United States has a completely different system, made up of a patchwork of more than 10,000 banks and savings and loans. What Canadians lose in diversity and competitiveness, they gain in stability. The collapse of hundreds of savings and loans cost American taxpayers hundreds of billions of dollars. Though we've had dozens of trust companies fail in the last couple of decades, at a cost of billions to financial institutions and the taxpayer (because of federal deposit insurance), we didn't have a bank failure between the collapse of the Home Bank in 1923, and the Canadian Commercial Bank, Northland Bank and Bank of British Columbia in 1985-86. In any case, it's clear that Ottawa would not allow one of the big chartered banks to fail.

There is a lot of debate over how competitive the banks really are. After all, they constitute an oligopoly (control by a few) dominated by five players (or six, if you include the much smaller National Bank) that compete on product and service – and much more narrowly on price. In fact, in a small market like Canada, five powerful players is quite a few. (For example, the beer, steel and airline industries each have two major competitors.) What matters is that there is enough competition among the banks to make it worthwhile to compare what they offer and to shop around.

The numbers behind Canada's banking system are staggering:
• 7,700 branches and 12,100 automated banking machines or ABMs (also called ATMs or automated teller machines) across the country, including Yukon and the Northwest Territories;
• 2.2 billion transactions a year, worth $18.4 trillion;
• 173,000 employees, most of them women;
• 25 million Visa and MasterCard bank cards, almost one per Canadian;
• 85 per cent of the country's outstanding small business loans;
• $34 billion in mutual fund assets, triple their market share in 1987;
• $148 billion in mortgage loans.

In 1993, the banks paid 15.5 per cent of all corporate income and capital taxes in Canada. The publicly traded banks make up 13.2 per cent of the weighting of the Toronto Stock Exchange 300 composite index. Each of the Big Five is in the top dozen most heavily weighted stocks. (National Trustco, the parent of National Trust, is the only remaining trust company on the TSE and makes up a minuscule 0.17 per cent of the index.)

The big banks make lots of money, though not nearly as much as the better American banks. In 1993, Bell Canada made corporate Canada's largest profit, $871 million. It was followed by CIBC, at $730 million, Bank of Nova Scotia at $714 million and Bank of Montreal at $709 million (all figures are in Canadian dollars), distantly followed by Seagram, the whisky people, at $379 million (U.S.). These profits both gratify and embarrass the banks. The Royal Bank had to deploy some accounting legerde-

main in 1991 to avoid reaching the all-too-visible $1 billion prof-
it level; it managed to finagle the figure down to $983 million.

Similarly enlightening were the salaries of the bank's senior
executives, made public for the first time in late 1993, thanks to
a change in the law in Ontario. Leading the list was Bank of
Montreal chairman Matthew Barrett, with total compensation of
$1.75 million for the year. At least the Bank of Montreal had a
good year; more questionable were the earnings of chairman
Dick Thomson of the TD, which did not. TD stumbled through
its third consecutive poor year, yet Thomson is thought to have
(again) taken home a $600,000 bonus, bringing his total com-
pensation to $1.525 million. The bank refused to reveal execu-
tive bonuses for 1993 but, under intense pressure from angry
shareholders at its January 1994 annual meeting, agreed to do so
in future. By American standards, these numbers are modest.

Canada's big banks have greatly expanded their reach in the
last decade and will continue to move closer to their goal of providing "one-stop financial shopping" for consumers. As a recent
cover story in *United States Banker* pointed out, "nationwide banking, the ability to own insurers and securities firms, large concentrated retail systems – the fantasy of many American bankers
can be found in Canada today."[1]

The banks' growing share of the financial services industry
becomes apparent when one compares the industry's four traditional "pillars": the banks, the trust companies, the insurance
companies and the investment dealers (brokers). The trust industry has melted away over the last decade, the victim of misman-
agement, overexpansion, non-arm's-length dealings with aggressive corporate owners, and huge losses on real estate loans. The
banks have swallowed up billions of dollars of the trust industry's
assets and have set up their own trust subsidiaries. (The Royal
Bank took over Royal Trust's assets, Bank of Nova Scotia bought

Montreal Trust, the Laurentian Bank acquired branches of Standard Trust, General Trust and Prenor Trust, the National Bank bought General Trust's Quebec branches, and TD bought Central Guaranty Trust Co., backed by guarantees of $3.7 billion from the Canada Deposit Insurance Corp. – in other words, depositors and taxpayers.)

In 1987, the banks were allowed to buy Bay Street investment dealers. They responded with a buying spree, right at the top of the market (in at least one case, just in time for the October crash). The Royal bought Dominion Securities and renamed it RBC Dominion Securities; CIBC bought Wood Gundy; Bank of Montreal took over Nesbitt Thomson; Scotiabank bought McLeod Weir Young and formed ScotiaMcLeod; the National bought Lévesque Beaubien (now Lévesque Beaubien Geoffrion). TD was the only major bank not to join in, choosing instead to establish its own brokerage, discount broker Green Line Investor Services. Three American-controlled firms dropped out of the running. Merrill Lynch sold its retail operations to Wood Gundy, and Dean Witter Reynolds' operations went to Midland Walwyn, while Prudential-Bache packed up its bags and abandoned the Canadian market entirely.

That left only three significant non-bank players for retail investors: Burns Fry, Midland Walwyn (Mackenzie Financial Corp., the mutual fund company, is its largest shareholder) and family-owned Richardson Greenshields. Three became two in July 1994, when the Bank of Montreal announced it would pay $403 million for Burns Fry and merge it with Nesbitt Thomson, thereby creating Nesbitt Burns, the country's largest investment dealer with $28 billion in assets. A day later the Laurentian Bank and Midland Walwyn announced they were striking a strategic alliance, which further consolidated the bank-broker marriages.

As brokers expand their product ranges, they are providing an alternative to the banks, or as much of an alternative as is possible in an industry that is largely bank-controlled. Competition is also coming from insurance companies, the financial arms of the auto companies and retailers who offer their own credit cards.

Federal legislation passed in 1992 eliminated most of the remaining barriers separating the pillars. Lobbying from the insurance industry, however, thwarted the banks' attempts to obtain the right to sell insurance through their branch networks (some say Tory prime minister Brian Mulroney was influenced by the views of his friend Paul Desmarais, the head of Power Corp., which owns Great-West Life Assurance Co.). That hasn't prevented CIBC from setting up its own insurance subsidiary, which it expects will have revenues of $500 million by 1998. Other banks are joining the fray. It's widely expected that the banks will get the right to sell insurance from their branches when the Bank Act faces its regular review in 1997.

The banks are also increasingly moving into money management. CIBC announced in January 1994 that it was joining forces with Montreal-based TAL Investment Counsel Ltd. to create a new firm under TAL's name, with $20 billion in pension and mutual fund assets. This is also occurring through the banks' trust arms. Royal Bank now owns Royal Trust's substantial money-management arm.

In short, the big banks already control much of three of the pillars (banks, trusts and investment dealers), appear poised to win a good chunk of the fourth (insurance), and are expanding into money management, which one observer has described as a fifth pillar. Canada Trust, which has a good reputation, is the only trust company left that is big enough to compete head to head with the banks. It effectively operates like a bank, even though its ownership is much different. (Through its holding company, it's 98 per cent owned by Montreal-based Imasco Ltd., which also owns Imperial Tobacco and Shoppers Drug Mart. Domestically owned banks, by comparison, have to be widely held, with no shareholder owning more than 10 per cent.) Canada Trust desperately wants to become a bank, and hopes to do so after the next revisions to the Bank Act. National Trust is the last remaining healthy mid-size trust. It has long been thought that it will eventually be sold by its majority owner, Hal Jackman, Ontario's lieutenant-governor, to a bank, most likely CIBC.

Don't expect any serious competitors to the banks to appear anytime soon. Foreign banks, since they arrived *en masse* in the mid-1980s, have had a tough time establishing niches here, let alone making any money. Some have given up and left. The barriers to entry are too great, with ownership restrictions, the enormous capital requirements and the strength of the competition.

The Good, the Bad and the Ugly

This is not a bank-bashing book. Bashing the banks is easy, simplistic and of little value to those who have to deal with these powerful, imperfect institutions. Nor is *How to Get What You Want From Your Bank* an apology for the banks, though it does try to represent their views fairly and to explain their thinking. Rather, the approach is one of healthy skepticism, as it should be for any institution that impinges so heavily on our lives and spends a fortune on presenting an agreeable public face.

The criticisms of the banks are well known, no more so than by the banks themselves. Virtually everyone has a bank horror story or knows someone who has. Because of their ability to deny credit, bankers will never be loved, no matter what they do. At best, they will be viewed – like dentists or undertakers – as a necessary evil.

The opinion of media mogul Conrad Black, who has had his own bad experiences with Canadian banks, is hard to fault. "I think the banking system has a very undistinguished record in this country, and indeed in most countries in the last few years," he told me in November 1993. "They made countless billions of dollars of bad loans following each other around, in a manner that was really highly irresponsible – and how reluctant they are to pay the price for it in the higher executive levels, where the responsibility must ultimately reside." Over the last dozen years, the banks have written off billions in loans to Third World countries, Dome Petroleum, Campeau Corp. and the Reichmann family's Olympia & York Developments Ltd., to name only a few of their most notable disasters. In the Reichmanns' case, it's clear that the banks didn't follow the most elementary loan criteria, such as insisting upon complete access to financial statements.

And who was one of the leaders of the charge to lend to Olympia & York? Al Flood, who was rewarded for his efforts by being promoted to the chairmanship of CIBC (1993 compensation: $1.5 million, including a bonus of $704,000). So much for accountability. "I was obviously a participant in that team [that agreed to make the loans] and I accept my responsibility for that," Flood said after the 1993 annual meeting. "On the other hand, we have made plenty of other decisions, that have not always been reported, that were positive in terms of how we manage these relationships."[2] That sounds credible until you look at the numbers. Thanks to the $1.2 billion CIBC lent to the Reichmanns, it had to increase its provisions for bad loans in 1992 to $1.8 billion, more than a billion dollars higher than the previous year. Despite bank denials, all these bad loans ultimately affect the banks' ordinary customers, who are bound to pay more for their loans and services.

Nor did the banks' free enterprise philosophy prevent them from going to Parliament Hill in Ottawa and Queen's Park in Toronto, the home of the Ontario government, with their hands outstretched, begging governments to bail them – and the Reichmanns – out of the mess they had created. For once, the governments made the right decision: they said they would not try to resolve a private-sector problem by using taxpayers' dollars.

These are the same banks that issue finger-wagging brochures to consumers about financial responsibility and prudent financial management. And as discussed in the small business chapter, they are the same banks that make small business people sign their lives away to borrow $50,000 and have been known to cut off lines of credit even when loan payments are being made on time.

Ironically, while they have an aversion to the risks of small business lending, the banks increasingly embrace the far greater risks – with much larger sums of money – of derivatives (complex financial contracts whose value derives from changes in the value of an underlying asset, such as a currency).

All this said, in many ways the banks are improving. One of the sad ironies is that they have improved in part because of vigorous competition from trust companies, most of which are now gone. For example, the banks dropped their antiquated hours – including closing at 3:30 p.m. – only in response to the initiative of Canada Trust in the mid-1970s.

Bank product ranges are also better than they used to be. Competition is more intense, and there is a genuine desire to respond to consumer needs (something I saw in the bankers I interviewed). Those needs are determined, in part, from focus groups. The latest round of major lending disasters and write-offs appears to be behind them.

Still, there is a serious gap in this general improvement, which the banks are trying to remedy. They lack a well-informed, flexible, motivated staff at the branch level that has some authority. There is here a legacy of history: a rulebook mentality, an authoritarian structure, poor pay, and its inevitable consequence – high turnover. That turnover has also been caused by the banks' frequent and arbitrary transfer of branch managers – a practice that is lessening – coupled with those managers' ambitions to move to head office or to larger centres. One hopes that as more responsive executives take over – "Mr. Goodbank," Bank of Montreal chairman Matthew Barrett, is the most widely cited example – the quality of staff will improve more rapidly (the bank has just opened a $40-million learning centre in Scarborough, Ontario). Eventually, however, the need for talented people at the branch level may diminish as more banking is done electronically.

Barrett put his finger on part of the problem when he talked – refreshingly – about why people go into banking in the first place. "I think everyone backs into banking," he said on CBC's "Morningside" in February 1994. "I mean, have you ever met a child that you [asked]: What do you want to be when you grow up? And they say, you know, I want to be a banker. I mean get real. People want to be pilots or firemen or policemen. Almost everyone I have ever met started out wanting to be something else."

Bankers do seem to have developed a greater sense of social responsibility, of realizing the consequences of calling a line of credit or shutting down a business. They know they have a bad reputation, and most of them are working to improve it, either for its own sake or because they know it's better for business and more in keeping with the times.

At the most senior levels of the banks, there has long been a fear that if their actions or policies become too much at odds with the perceived public good, governments will regulate them more closely. That fear is most apparent during parliamentary inquiries on banking issues. It's no coincidence that these inquiries tend to coincide with bank initiatives: witness the spate of announcements (such as TD's reduction of the personal guarantees required under the Small Business Loans Act) early in 1994, just as the House of Commons' Industry Committee was preparing to grill bank executives on small business loans. Fear of regulation is one of the reasons the banks are so sensitive to criticism, whether from politicians, consumer groups or the media.

Because of their dominant position, banks in Canada find themselves in an unusual position. They believe their greatest, if not their only, responsibility is to their shareholders. Yet governments, interest groups and the public expect them to serve the greater good, and to be answerable to a broad range of constituencies. Hence the view of more radical critics such as small business person Susan Bellan. "I am always being told by my bank that my loan is a privilege and not a right," she told MPs. "I think we have to make it clear to banks that their charters are a privilege and not a right."[3] She suggests charters should come up for renewal every five years, and that banks be regulated in the same way that utilities with dominant positions, like Bell Canada, are regulated. In her view, the banks should have to show they are using the benefits bestowed upon them by their charters to invest in their communities, lend a certain amount to small business and create jobs.

The Future

A bank is an intermediary, paying depositors for funds and then lending those funds out to those same depositors, and to others, at a higher rate. The difference or spread is their margin, which pays the bank's expenses and provides a profit. Increasingly, bank profits are not coming from interest rate spreads, which have shrunk because of competition for depositors, who have demanded higher returns. Even less are they coming from corporate loans, which have proven to be poorly priced and too risky (in any case, companies are finding it cheaper to raise money in the capital markets than to borrow from the banks).

Rather, profits are coming – and will continue to come – from fees and services. There are fees now for just about everything, from transferring an account to applying for a small business loan. That has intensified the courting of the domestic bank customer, a boon for savvy consumers. That trend should continue.

So should the move towards electronic banking, particularly since one of the banks' biggest advantages (besides their financial strength, ability to raise funds cheaply from depositors and coast-to-coast branch networks) is their computer systems and databases. Whether those networks will remain a big advantage – as banking by machine, phone, home computer and television becomes more common – remains to be seen. CIBC recently unveiled a flagship "bank of the future" in downtown Toronto, and personal bank president Holger Kluge proudly asked, "Do you see any tellers? – No, there are none." Instead, there were 38 banking machines. Technology will make banking easier in the future, but will lead to a new set of problems. Security and the privacy of financial information will increasingly become issues, as we shall see in Chapter 8.

This emphasis upon the domestic bank customer means that the bank wants and needs your business. It wants to establish a banking relationship, to get as many of your assets under its control as possible, and it is willing to make concessions in a competitive marketplace in order to do so. That's good news for the well-informed customer willing to compare the options available and to negotiate the best deal. And that's why, as I hope the following pages will show, you *can* get what you want from your bank.

*Capitalism without bankruptcy
is like Christianity
without Hell.*

FRANK BORMAN, FORMER CEO,
EASTERN AIR LINES INC.

*If you go across the country,
you can lose yourself in this society,
as long as you don't apply for credit.*

FBI AGENT JOHN GULLEY, WHO NABBED GEORGIA
EMBEZZLER MALCOLM CHEEK WITH THE HELP OF A BANK
THAT PURSUED CHEEK FOR DELINQUENT CAR PAYMENTS

CHAPTER 1

PERSONAL CREDIT: HOW TO GET IT AND LOSE IT

Begging You to Borrow

"We're paying attention," the Bank of Montreal earnestly intones in its advertisements. And, indeed, the bank *is* paying attention. Just set up a Personal Line of Credit, let it lie fallow for a while, and you'll probably get a letter like this one, received by my wife:

"I've noticed that you haven't used your Personal Line of Credit recently, and I wanted to write and remind you of its many advantages for using its potential. As a Bank of Montreal Personal Line of Credit customer, you have access to funds, up to your approved credit limit, anytime you want, for any reason! ... No need to reapply, all you have to do is to use it."

While the letter goes on to suggest reasons for borrowing – home renovations, new car, taking a vacation, paying off bills – the emphasis is clearly on borrowing, almost for its own sake, rather than having a compelling reason to borrow.

Or how about this example of the bank paying attention, in a letter to one of my colleagues at *The Globe and Mail*:

"I am writing to tell you about a new loan option that could put money back into your pocket every month for a full year. Extra cash that you could use to repay other higher interest obligations you may have, take a vacation, or for any other purpose that's important to you. Now, for a limited time, you are eligible to make interest only payments on a personal loan at Bank of Montreal – for one full year."

The bank is offering to "put money back into your pocket." If you take up its offer, however, it will actually take more from your pocket. Say you have a $10,000, three-year loan at 10.25 per cent. Your normal payment would be $323.85 a month, and your borrowing costs would be $1,659. The bank says that by paying interest only, you will have $238.43 "extra cash available every month" for a year. Though it's not in the letter, you would pay $85.42 a month for the first year and then $462.60 for the next 24 months. Your borrowing costs are $2,127, almost $500 more than the normal arrangement.

These are the same banks that issue scolding brochures about responsible borrowing and the horrors of a poor credit history.

The moral? Always remember that at the end of the day your bank is trying to sell you products, in this case, loans. Financial institutions and retailers are competing to entice the more than 10 million Canadians they consider creditworthy to borrow and to buy. That's fine; that's the business they're in. But it's up to you to ensure that borrowing that money and buying that product are really in your own best interest.

It's a bit reminiscent of the liquor companies, which talk out of both sides of their very wide mouths. Don't drink and drive. Drink in moderation. Don't drink if you're pregnant. But whatever you do, drink. Buy as many of our fine products as you can cram into the trunk of your car, or into a taxi, if you can't afford a car.

Liquor companies and financial institutions both have an image problem. The difference is that while the liquor companies get blamed for some of the ill consequences of drinking, they don't bear those consequences themselves. Banks, on the other hand, do share the consequences of irresponsible borrowing. They might not get their money back, and they, like the debtor, can go through a mild version of purgatory in their struggle to settle a bad account.

The bottom line? Credit, like alcohol, is best used in moderation. Borrow as little as you can; borrow to fulfill needs rather than wants. Don't be lulled by the sophistry of the CIBC Credit Smart Guide, which says, "Borrowing allows you to enhance your lifestyle today with money you will earn in the future." Or the money you'll have when your $20 stock goes to $30. The problem, of course, is that you may be earning less in the future and your stock could fall, rather than rise.

Boomers Take a Bath

Anyone who has read a newspaper in the last four years knows that the worst can indeed happen to you or to someone you know. A reasonable debt level can turn overnight into an intolerable burden when you lose a job you thought was secure. Or your spouse could lose his or her job, with the result that credit granted on two incomes must now, uneasily, be supported by one.

No one is immune. A Liberal MP (and lawyer, no less), elected for the first time in 1993 for a southwestern Ontario riding, and her husband were sued for defaulting on personal debts of more than $200,000. They had remortgaged their home four times, bounced cheques, and choked on a personal loan – from a priest. In Montreal, meanwhile, a court ordered the seizure of goods valued at $1 million from a member of the Birks family, which founded the jewellery chain, after he defaulted on a $1-million personal loan.

Consumer debt regained its pre-recession peak in August 1993. Canadians were borrowing more because they were earning less, thanks to low wage settlements, high levels of unemployment and spiraling taxes. We are mimicking our beleaguered governments with our debts.

Total household debt, including mortgages, grew all the way

to $461 billion in 1992. That's a record high $14,400 per Canadian or 86 per cent of our total after-tax income, compared with 50 per cent only 10 years ago. But if Canadians are borrowing more, they're enjoying it less, certainly less than they did in the 1980s. They realize the days of the impulse purchase, the leveraged investment in real estate or stocks, the unneeded BMW, are largely over. More Canadians are now aware that the prudent thing to do – the financial equivalent of sensible shoes – is to pay down debt, not add to it.

In March 1992, Canadians set a record of 76,000 consumer and business bankruptcies. In the United States, a multi-state study showed the face of bankruptcy was changing. Baby boomers, who make up 44 per cent of the American adult population, accounted for 59 per cent of personal bankruptcies. "Baby boomers are part of the 'me generation'," said one of the authors of the 1993 study. "They weren't chastened by the Depression. It is a combination of consumerism and optimism that could put them at risk of bankruptcy." Sound familiar?

Closer to home, business at the Credit Counselling Service of Metropolitan Toronto, one of 800 such offices across North America, has been brisk. The branch served 6,150 troubled clients over the year ending in March 1994, up almost 50 per cent from the previous year. New clients on average had annual incomes of $27,600, faced $15,500 in debts, and had six creditors pounding at their doors, often quite literally. Utter the words "credit problems" and 99 out of 100 times you can add two more words: "credit cards." This form of credit has pitfalls of its own, as we will see in a later chapter.

Bankers and credit counsellors say it's amazing to see who ends up in credit trouble: people right across the social and economic spectrum, including an increasing number with good salaries and educations. "They may have a university degree," says Laurie Campbell, program manager for Toronto's Credit Counselling Service, "they may have higher education, but they still don't know how to manage their money properly."

Nightmare on Credit Street: Credit Bureaus

You probably haven't heard of them, but they will certainly have heard of you. In fact, they know an awful lot about you – your social insurance number, your employer, the last time you ran to the bank machine a day late to pay your Visa – and are happy to share the information with those who grant credit. The "they" I'm referring to is a company called Equifax Canada, which has the market for personal credit information in this country locked up (Dun & Bradstreet has the equivalent position for business credit information).

If you, like millions of others, have been a bit slipshod in managing your financial affairs, but have resolved to get them in good working order, you can do no better than to start by paying Equifax a visit. Or you can write or phone them (check the phone book for a 1-800 number) to find out what delicious information they have on you. It's particularly useful if you are hoping to arrange a large loan, or your status has recently changed because of a divorce or the death of a spouse. It's essential if you want to establish credit in your own name, rather than in your spouse's. Those who are working their way out of credit trouble should make sure any agreements made with creditors are on their file.

You will be able to see much of what the bank sees on a terminal in the branch, when you ask for credit. You have a legal right to look at your file, and depending on the province, you can see it either for nothing or for a nominal fee.

Your file will contain basic personal information, though no comments, a list of credit grantors that have asked to see your file, details on each of your credit positions, including loans and credit cards (including corporate credit cards with your name on them), and any debt default judgments against you. It will normally not include information about not sufficient funds (NSF) cheques or overdrafts, unless you have overdraft protection, which requires an application for credit.

Your file will not include any record of your accounts with utilities, the phone company, student loans, or the tax people, unless there is action being taken against you or there is a judgment against you. Nor will it normally include mortgage information, largely because mortgages are always backed by seizable collateral, in the form of your house or property.

(Equifax Canada's director of quality assurance, Lawrence Brown, told me that in such an aggressive marketplace, he has a personal concern about including mortgage information, including the maturity date, in files. He is afraid of the scenario where you are applying for a loan and the loans officer takes a peek at your file and says, "Oh, I see your Royal Trust mortgage is due in seven months. Can I sell you a mortgage?" And financial institutions do not want to put their client information in a file that their competitors can see.)

I have a copy of my own Equifax file in front of me, and it shows (correctly) that I have had a personal line of credit with a limit of $10,000 at the Bank of Montreal since February 1990. The balance at the end of the latest month is $2,779 and my current rating is R1, the highest available (R1 means you pay within 30 days of the due date or are not more than one payment past due).

The R scale descends to R9, credit hell (bad debt, placed for collection). The file will show the most recent month's rating for a credit facility, such as a credit card, and a record of the worst rating you have ever had with that facility. While financial institutions do show some flexibility, particularly if they know you, too many R2s (pays in more than 30 but less than 60 days, or not more than two payments past due) and R3s (pays in 60 to 90 days, or not more than three payments past due), particularly recent ones, will send up a red flag.

I discovered that I have a five-and-a-half-year-old R2 on a MasterCard. I would like to think I was late because the bill fell down the back of the fridge or the dog ate it (okay, I don't have a dog). Most provincial records go back only six years, so that "derog" (derogatory piece of information) will soon be erased. Bankruptcies stay on for seven years. Your Equifax file doesn't contain an overall credit rating.

I also arranged to see my file on a terminal in the collections department in the Bay Street head office of one of the big banks. The file was much fuller and slightly different from the one Equifax gave me and was arranged according to the institution's particular system and criteria. It did, for example, have a section (fortunately blank, in my case) for NSF cheques. It also included an overall score, according to a "Beacon" system developed by Equifax. Though each institution decides what it considers a good score, 400 is usually considered the depths of deadbeatism and 800 is great. My score was 757, just enough to edge out my wife (723).

Although this score is only one part of the bank's assessment of your creditworthiness, it was used to "pre-approve" people for the recently introduced TD GM Visa card. That card "is pushing up against the wall in my particular belief," said Paul Vessey, senior vice-president of card products for CIBC, which issues the competing Ford Visa card, in an interview. "Here it is, sign here, and you get it. The TD GM card has been successful not only because it's free, but also because it's been pre-approved. TD has taken a Beacon score against a list of names that it has bought.

"Now that's a hell of a risky proposition to get into," continues Mr. Vessey, "because Beacon scores are not as predictive as one would like, and I think my friend Mr. [David] Livingston [TD's Visa chief] and General Motors are taking a hell of a risk on the credit risk side, but that's my opinion. It's not something I would recommend to our shareholders."

If you apply for credit and your credit history is not up to snuff, the banks say they are required to tell you only that they have a negative credit report and may send you off to the credit bureau to survey the damage yourself. This year 600,000 to 800,000 Canadians will check their Equifax files. The largest percentage go out of curiosity, and the next largest because they have credit problems.

Remember that the credit bureau simply collects and inputs information, accurate or inaccurate, from credit grantors. It does not make credit assessments, so it can't tell you why your request has been declined. That's the job of those who grant credit. So if you are refused a loan or credit card, get the reasons for the refusal in writing. The bureau will go through your file with you, which should make clear which credit grantor is causing you the problem. Remember, too, that the onus is on you to make sure the information in your file is correct. It hardly seems fair, but that's the way it is.

Credit bureaus have been heavily criticized, particularly in the United States, for the high percentage of mistakes in credit files. Estimates are that between a third and a half of all files contain incorrect information, ranging from the trivial to the damning. Congress is mulling over bills that would force bureaus to reduce the level of errors (one critic entitled his submission to Congress, "Don't Call, Don't Write, We Don't Care").

In this country, the CBC program "Market Place" had 100 people check their files and found that 47 per cent contained errors of one kind or another, and 13 per cent had mistakes that could affect an individual's access to credit. While credit bureaus are the leading source of consumer complaints south of the border, they generate few complaints here. As I discovered through a Freedom of Information request, there were 306 complaints and inquiries to the government of Ontario in 1993. That was miles behind the frontrunners, which were motor vehicle sales (2,193) and repairs (1,750). That could be because Equifax, which is based in Atlanta, Georgia, does a better job here, because we have far fewer credit grantors and hence less data, or because Canadians complain less.

It's easy to uncover horror stories involving mistaken identity. Our former next-door neighbour in Toronto, Robert Sutherland, a trumpet player for the Canadian Opera who is now with the Metropolitan Opera in New York, was incorrectly listed by Equifax as 58 years old (which was wrong by 17 years), as the owner of a Simpsons' charge card since 1967 (when he was 15 and had no credit history), and as a former employee of the Salvation Army. "Can you imagine me working for the Salvation Army with my wine cellar?" he asks in amusement. Bob was told these references were data entry errors.

"So many data entry errors on a document so many institutions put so much weight on!" he says. "I would certainly advise everyone periodically to review their credit information, whether they need credit or not."

Try beating this story, however. In 1991, TRW, one of the big three credit bureaus in the United States (alongside Equifax and Trans Union), rated all 1,400 taxpayers of the affluent town of Norwich, Vermont, as deadbeats, including the doctors, lawyers, and judges. Ironically, Disney uses Norwich in its theme parks as a model New England town. TRW had sent a local housewife named Margaret Herr to the town office to compile a list of delinquent taxpayers. Instead, she wrote down the names of *all* taxpayers. A spokesman for the credit bureau dismissed the furore with the remark that "no huge number, probably less than

3,000 people" were hurt by the mistake, a remarkable comment since the town's total population was 3,100. And a lousy credit rating can turn your hitherto placid existence into a nightmare.

"I'm not suggesting we're squeaky clean, by any means," says Equifax's Lawrence Brown. "We're like everybody else, we make mistakes. But under the law they can be rectified, and rectified quickly, and they are." Brown disputes the percentages broadcast by "Market Place" and says almost all mistakes involve personal information, which is often not up to date. That seldom affects creditworthiness. Indeed, in my own case the credit information was correct (though my employer was listed as CBC "Business World," which I had left two years earlier). Mr. Brown said my file would not have been updated because I hadn't applied for credit in the last two years. He concedes that there are sometimes mistakes if names are similar – if, for example, a Lawrence Brown Sr. and Jr. lived at the same address.

"Credit repair" firms can't do anything you can't do yourself, even though their healthy charges might suggest otherwise. Equifax will give you an update form to fill out if you tell them the information in your file is inaccurate. If the file is correct but there are special circumstances, such as unemployment or a death in the family, you can add that in a "narrative" to your file. Mr. Brown says straightforward information that's wrong should be changed within 24 hours – five days at the most, if it's more complicated.

Critics blame the credit bureaus for the large number of mistakes. Mr. Brown argues that "everybody" needs to share the blame, including financial institutions (who submit the information), the bureaus (who input it), and borrowers, who, he says, often provide incomplete information on their applications. If you can't get satisfaction, complain to your provincial ministry of consumer affairs.

How to Get and Keep a Good Credit Rating

A lot of personal finance books and bank brochures suggest you need to have been an active user of credit, particularly credit cards, in order to build up a good credit rating.

"I find that to be somewhat of a joke," says Laurie Campbell of Toronto's Credit Counselling Service. "My own experience has been that I've had one card with a $500 limit, and it's never held me back from getting a mortgage or anything. There's no reason that you need all this credit. That's the big thing that clients come in with: I wanted to establish my credit rating. Well, six cards later, they're in here and they're in trouble."

"It was the oldest marketing ploy that we used 25 years ago," adds executive director Duke Stregger, a 35-year veteran of Sears Canada, where he was corporate general manager of credit. "Let's be honest. It was one of the things we used to get people to shop. Get a credit card in their hands and they'd be shopping in your store."

Most of the advice about keeping a good credit record is probably no different from what our mothers told us when we were kids:

• Plan ahead, so you are not caught totally offside if you lose your job or face unexpected expenses.

• Keep a realistic budget.

• Distinguish between needs and wants.

• Avoid impulse purchases.

• Borrow only when you need to. Your total monthly debt payments, including your mortgage, should be no more than 35 to 40 per cent of your gross monthly income. (I'll discuss this total debt service ratio further in the chapter on mortgages.)

• Try to save 10 per cent of your net income. (Good luck on this one. I have yet to meet a person who does. According to one

estimate, 41 per cent of Canadians would run out of money in a
month if their income was eliminated.)
• Contribute to an RRSP. It's a good way to save, particularly
since it's tax deductible.
• Pay your bills on time. Though it's very expensive to pay only
the minimum balance, doing so will at least keep creditors at bay,
if you're having credit problems. Pay the minimum, even if it's
tiny. I once ignored the monthly minimum on a personal line of
credit, because it barely exceeded the cost of a stamp, and the
computer red-flagged my name.
• Limit the number of credit cards you carry and use. Cut them up
if you can't handle them (I've even seen it suggested that you freeze
them into an ice-cube tray until you restore order to your finances).
Virtually everyone who walks in the door of a credit counselling
office has been wounded by the shrapnel of plastic explosives. A
plain vanilla Visa or MasterCard is all most people need.

All this is pretty obvious – if it isn't, paste this page to your
refrigerator. But here's something less obvious. You have six
credit cards but think there's no problem because you never use
four of them. Wrong. When a banker looks at your file, he or she
sees the *potential* for trouble. You have a combined credit limit of
$30,000, and here you are in the branch asking for a car loan.
The solution? Simple. Cancel any cards you don't use. But keep
a personal line of credit open in case you lose your job or
encounter unforeseen expenses.

Scenes From a Marriage: How to Get Credit in Your Own Name

Suppose your spouse or partner has a second credit card and
gives it to you to use. It even has your name on it. But you have
never applied for credit in your own name. Do you have credit?
You do not.

The credit bureau now has individual rather than joint files.

However, if you have credit in your own name but have ever taken out any joint credit with your spouse, such as a personal line of credit in both names, your names will be on each other's file.

The key principle is this. If you want to be treated as an individual, apply for credit as an individual, not as someone's spouse or partner. Many people want credit in their own name as a sign of their independence. But it makes practical sense, too. If you've been riding on the coattails of your spouse's credit and then split up, you will be left with no credit standing of your own. It will be tough to establish it then, at the very time you need it most.

If you don't have credit in your own name, ask the credit bureau to set up a file in your name. Contact all credit grantors directly and ask them to do the same thing. If you want to go beyond having your own file to having your own credit, you will probably have to have a job, or enough income of your own.

You are free to leave blank any section on a credit application that asks for details about your spouse, unless you are relying on his or her income or assets. If you do complete it, you should tell your spouse, because some credit grantors may then feel free to review both files (the appropriateness of this at a time when privacy is a concern is now being debated). The corollary of all this is that you cannot apply for credit as an individual and expect your income as a couple to be taken into account.

Certainly there are advantages to joint credit, where the agreement is co-signed and hence guaranteed by both spouses. You can include the incomes and assets of both of you on credit applications. If your partner pulls the plug, however, you could be stuck with some of his or her liabilities. Curiously, if you have a joint credit card and your partner dies, you can assume his or her credit rating, if the income flow on which it was based survives.

You are responsible for your spouse's debts only to the extent that you have joint property or if they are for clear necessities –

in other words, for the repairs to the leaky roof, but not to your spouse's BMW. Banks can sue only the person whose signature is on a credit agreement. The fact that you are married to a financial deadbeat shouldn't affect your personal credit rating. You can even withdraw the right of your spouse to use your credit by notifying the creditor.

How Do You Score?

If you're creditworthy, the bank wants to lend you money. Of course, the bank wants to be as certain as it can that it will get its money back. While loan losses on personal loans run around 1 per cent (they were higher during the recession), at least one major bank has a goal of reducing those losses by 1996 to 0.5 per cent. It doesn't bother to mention that that means it will have to be even more cautious about who it lends to.

How do banks assess whether you're a good credit risk for a loan or a credit card? Banks traditionally lend according to the "Five Cs of Credit" – though I've seen as few as three and as many as seven listed. Two "Cs" rely heavily on the judgment of the individual loans officer: Capacity, the ability to repay, and Character, the willingness to repay, which can usually be determined from your credit history. Then there's Capital, or your net worth (assets minus liabilities), and Collateral, the assets securing the loan against default. There's another "C" for business loans: Conditions, referring to the economic climate.

(A Scotiabank manager's briefing on commercial credit notes that "the traditional Five Cs of credit were not able to keep us out of the commercial real estate mess, the HLT [highly leveraged transaction] loan problems or any of the other lending fiascoes of the last 30 years." It goes on to list the Five Cs of *Bad* Credit. They are Complacency: "It's always worked out before;" Carelessness: "I wouldn't worry about it;" Communications: "You know what I mean;" Contingencies: "Hey, what can go wrong;" and Competition: "What it takes to win," regardless of the merits of the deal.)

Increasingly, however, lenders rely less upon the Five Cs than upon "credit scoring" (especially for credit cards), which they say has a good track record. "It's the wave of the future," a senior banker told me. It's particularly useful for smaller loans, because it means the bank doesn't have to spend a long time making a credit decision on a loan that will yield a small return. Credit scoring is used by all major credit grantors, including credit and charge card issuers, auto financing companies, and airlines for their travel cards.

The system was devised 30 years ago in the United States and is the product of the study of thousands of borrowers. As the name implies, credit scoring is a numerical score that measures your creditworthiness or credit risk: basically, whether you are likely to repay what you owe. It is used because it is far faster and more objective and "scientific" than personal judgment. According to a book by one of the founders of the system, "Since scoring is a consistent and demonstrable process, many credit grantors were motivated to adopt scoring in part as a defence against a charge of discrimination."[1]

"There is good reason to keep the details of the scoring system from becoming public knowledge," the same book says, adding with a rhetorical flourish that if a system were made public, "how many fraudulent applications would appear? So far no lender has been willing to try to find out." [2] Well, here's our chance. A source within a Big Five bank gave me its loan scorecard, on condition I didn't name the bank.

(CIBC advertises a mini-scorecard and invites those interested "to calculate your borrowing power," suggesting that the amount you determine is what the bank will lend you. Maybe – but maybe not. As the footnote in smaller type says, " 'Borrowing

Power' is subject to normal credit criteria standards.")

The scorecard assigns points in 10 categories (and refers only to the loan applicant, and not to the co-applicant, except where noted). Here they are:

• Residential status. The highest score goes to home owners or buyers; the lowest to renters, who do even worse than those who live with their parents or relatives.

• Time with present employer. The longer the time, the higher your score. The retired share the highest score with those who have worked at least 15 years with the same employer.

• Chequing and savings accounts of the applicant and co-applicant. The highest score goes to those with both chequing and savings accounts at the lender's bank.

• Finance company loan references for the applicant and co-applicant. The highest score goes to those who have not borrowed from a finance company or acceptance company (a company that finances instalment credit purchases, such as cars for auto manufacturers and fridges for retailers). The explanation for this is simple. No one would pay those very high interest rates to Household Finance if their credit were any good. But some uses of finance companies are almost accidental, and more acceptable. If the Brick Warehouse finances your new stove, it will do so through a finance company.

• Time with the bank in question. The longer you've been with the bank, the higher your score, whether you have an account with $10 in it or $10 million.

• Purpose of the loan. Highly rated loans include those for RRSPs, real estate, autos, and renovations, and those backed by home equity. Loans for boats, RVs and motorcycles are less well rated.

• Number of credit inquiries within the last six months. The fewer, the better. The banks are on the lookout for frequent "credit seekers." A lot of inquiries from creditors suggests people are getting nervous about you.

• Average time in file. The longer you've had a credit file, the better.

• Worst credit bureau rating. A minor derogatory rating earns a slap on the wrist; two or more major derogs will get you a kick in the pants, or worse.

• Revolving debt as a percentage of your credit limit. The best scores are to modest users of credit (1 to 19 per cent); the worst have "maxed out" at the 80 per cent or higher level.

What does the scorecard tell us? That – surprise – banks love stability and reward you for having your own home, staying with the same employer, and being their customer. That they want to make certain you have a history of paying your bills. And that they want to know you haven't taken on more debt than you can handle.

In short, credit scoring is a way to attach a score to the Five Cs of Credit. Because the system eliminates personal judgment, it can unfairly categorize individuals. You might be a young renter in a new job, with little credit history and no relationship with a bank. You'll be penalized as a result, despite your fine personal attributes.

Since the bank considers the purpose of the loan when it makes its assessment, you will have a better chance of getting a loan to renovate and add value to your home than to purchase a Lamborghini Diablo. As Stephen Stewart, TD's vice-president of personal lending, neatly summarizes, "There are loans to acquire assets, there are loans to acquire toys, and there are loans to pay for past sins." You will pay more for toys and sins than you will to acquire assets.

Danger Signs

Major credit problems are worth avoiding. Why? Because the regimen you will eventually be forced to accept is about as much fun as Weight Watchers or AA.

Here's a list of the things the credit counselling people advise for miscreants: avoid buying snacks or "empty calorie" foods, use worn-out towels to make washcloths, cut out tobacco and alcohol, eliminate subscriptions to magazines that only entertain, get rid of one car, use the public library for reading materials, eliminate cable TV, and take vacations at home. I'm afraid it all sounds too worthy to me.

As with everything bad, from disease to profligacy, early detection is critical. The sooner you recognize a credit problem, admit it, and seek help for it, the easier it will be to resolve.

Here are a few of the danger signs that you are an overspender, compiled by the Credit Counselling Service of Metropolitan Toronto. Some of them may sound uncomfortably familiar:

• You are at or near the limit of your lines of credit.

• You can make only the minimum payments on your revolving charge accounts.

• You are chronically late in paying your bills.

• You are paying bills with money earmarked for something else.

• You are tapping your savings to pay current bills.

• You are putting off medical or dental visits because you can't afford to go.

• If you lost your job, you would find yourself in immediate financial difficulty.

• You are unsure how much you owe.

• You take cash advances on one credit card to pay off another.

• You spend over 20 per cent of your income on credit card bills.

• You are forced to pay for everyday items with a credit card.

• You often hide your credit card purchases from your family.

• You like to collect cash from friends in restaurants and then charge the tab to your card.

Reading this list, I wonder if I should send it anonymously to one of my best friends, who recently told me he was buying all his groceries at Shoppers Drug Mart because they accept credit cards.

Digging Yourself Out of Credit Hell

If you find yourself in financial difficulties, at some stage you will want to inform your bank, particularly if you have a good relationship. They have an interest in helping you to work out an arrangement, whether it's a modest change in the repayment schedule or a substantial refinancing. Sure, you're taking a risk by getting them involved. But it's better to phone them than wait for them to phone you, which will be soon enough if your repayment cheque doesn't arrive.

"I know it's sometimes hard to believe, but we are not this totally insensitive, business-oriented screw-the-customer type of institution," David Livingston, TD's senior vice-president, Visa, said during a discussion of the options available to someone who has lost his or her job and built up a lot of debt on credit cards. "We do call them and say: this is not the best way to do this. Take out a loan. Consolidate all your cash flow. If you've got a whole bunch of debt on your credit card, we would rather give you a loan. If you don't have a job and you've got no income, it's in our interest to lower your interest payments, as much as in your interest, and to spread out the payments."

And if you're in trouble, credit counsellors will advise you to keep your credit card paid up, he says. "If you're going to have to stiff somebody or do something or make a deal, do it on an asset, do it on a loan, don't do it on a card, because you need the card to live." (Credit counsellors say that while cards can be a lifeline for some people, too many others use them to avoid facing their financial problems.)

Bankers say they particularly try to show flexibility when towns that rely heavily upon one industry, such as Sudbury, Hamilton, or Nanaimo, are experiencing problems. It's not that bankers are sharing, caring people; rather, it's that the last thing they want to do is to push somebody over the brink. When that happens, creditors get nothing, or next to it.

Banks hate repossessing cars, or anything else. Increasingly, they use their own collection departments, because outsiders' fees often amount to half any proceeds raised. The returns on repossessed goods sold at auction are lousy. The bank will be lucky to end up with a small percentage of the total amount owed. Historically, the student loan people and Revenue Canada (which, until the bankruptcy laws were changed, was at the front of the line) are notorious for their zeal in getting their pound of flesh.

There is no set rule as to when the bank will come after you. I asked one banker when she considered a loan to be delinquent, innocently suggesting 30 days past due. "*One* day after it's due," she snapped.

(I have only once been phoned by a collection agency, about a tiny, long-forgotten bill I had apparently signed in my own name, rather than in the name of the magazine of which I was editor. I carefully explained this distinction to the collector, suggesting he contact the corporate owner. It was at that point that the collector, who began the conversation politely enough, replied with a bark, "That's all well and good, but *your* name is on the bill, so when are *you* going to pay it?")

A credit counselling service is a good option for someone with recurring credit problems. The federal bankruptcy legislation passed in 1992 makes it easier to work out a repayment schedule with creditors and easier to go bankrupt. Go to one of the 800 non-profit organizations across North America, not to a "made-for-profit" firm. Such firms are unregulated, charge a lot, and – unlike the non-profit services – may have no standing with creditors.

In Ontario, credit counsellors can set up a Debt Management

Program (also known as a voluntary Orderly Payment of Debt program) and deal with creditors on your behalf. In most cases, they can help you to clear your debts within 36 to 48 months, during which time you will not be allowed to use your credit cards or take out any loans without their permission. You will pay a small fee for counselling services, if you can afford it. In most other provinces, the programs are operated by the provincial consumer ministry.

Other options for escaping credit hell include informal proposals for settlement, whereby the debtor negotiates directly with creditors, and formal proposals, which can offer protection from lawsuits and property seizure. Bankruptcy trustees administer formal proposals on behalf of the debtor. Be aware that trustees have been known to guide clients towards bankruptcy, since the process is shorter and the fees higher. "It's like having the mouse guard the cheese," says one credit counsellor of the trustees.

Counsellors say that eight out of ten people they see are able to avoid bankruptcy, and only a small fraction of those who complete a Debt Management Plan get in credit trouble again.

Bankruptcy

Bankruptcy has been called the Seven-Year Mistake, because that's how long it will remain on your credit record. Though the stigma has been disappearing, as it has for divorce, it should be seen as a last resort. According to American studies, more women, especially single and divorced women, are declaring bankruptcy. More women are getting credit, but they tend to have less income and fewer assets than men, which leaves them with a lesser ability to cope with financial adversity.

The good news about declaring bankruptcy is that it will protect you from creditors who are thoughtfully providing you with those nightly wake-up calls. That is far outweighed by the bad news. Legally, the trustee is working not for you, but for your creditors. You will lose much of your property, be forced to pay fees to declare bankruptcy, and be obliged to tell all credit grantors about your declaration. You will still have to pay all alimony, support payments and court fines. You could have trouble getting credit for years to come.

Summary
- Use credit in moderation.
- Get a copy of your credit file, and make sure it's accurate and up to date.
- Get credit in your own name.
- Be aware of the credit danger signs.
- If you are having problems, talk to your bank and consider a non-profit credit counselling service.
- Declare bankruptcy only as an absolute last resort.

CHAPTER 2

PERSONAL LOANS

What Bank Customers Want

What do people want most when they walk into a branch to borrow money? The obvious answer is, "The lowest interest rate and the easiest and most flexible repayment terms."

Wrong, according to the banks' focus groups. What the banks learned is reflected in a Scotiabank brochure that shows a couple in an open, 1920s car with water up to the axles, stalled in the middle of a lake. The photo looks like a still from a silent-era, slapstick comedy.

"You won't feel stranded when you apply for a loan at Scotiabank," reads the headline over the car. "Whatever we do at Scotiabank," the copy inside reads, "comes out of a very single-minded philosophy: Make it easy for the customer. So when you come to us for a loan, there's nothing to unsettle you. And everything to welcome you."

"It's a very intimidating experience for most people to come in to apply for a loan," explains Stephen Stewart, TD's vice-president of personal lending. "So they want a relatively soft approach, they want to be made comfortable, they don't want to feel we're doing them a favour. They want to be treated like a customer who's requesting a service we want to sell them."

Pat Skene, vice-president of consumer credit for CIBC, adds, "We have found through focus groups that the most important thing to the client is how he's treated during the process, and the stress associated with 'Am I going to be approved?'... People walking in for a loan feel intimidated, feel they have failed in some way, that they are not in the driver's seat ... We're trying to turn that around. It's very important that the customer know that the banks do need the loan business."

People want the process to be simple and fast. That's why lenders now offer 1-800 numbers so that you can apply – almost anonymously, it seems – over the telephone in a pin-striped version of phone sex. You can get your answer in 24 hours.

This emphasis on speed has yielded some unfortunate results, such as this particularly dreadful ad: "It's TD for you, Sue/Get your loan-by-phone, Joan/See how you could win, Jin."

What the Bank Wants

Banks want to lend you money, if you're a creditworthy customer. Bankers make money by lending money, collecting the spread or differential between the cost of funds to them (as raised in the money markets and paid to depositors) and the interest you pay on loans. Contrary to what most people think, their spread (and hence profit) is usually greater when rates are low or falling. They can quickly drop what they pay to depositors while continuing to collect the old, high interest rates on fixed-rate loans. Banks also make money by charging fees, as they do with business lending. The greatest blow to a bank is to see a low-risk borrower walk out the door and head off to a competitor. Keep that in mind.

If your credit history is weak, a good relationship with a bank will help. If the branch has known you for a reasonable length of time, and if you or your family does a lot of business with it – deposits, RRSPs and mortgages – you will have both ties and leverage.

Your branch has some discretion in what it offers you. Loans officers usually have a target interest rate and a minimum rate, which is what you are aiming for. The branch will have a target return on its portfolio. My wife and I had a joint personal line of credit we didn't ask for and didn't want foisted upon us when we negotiated our mortgage. This made us victims, I suspect, of an eager banker's quota or ambitions.

If your debt is too high or the amount you want to borrow exceeds the branch limit, the loan decision will be made at a higher level, which means you will not be able to present your case in person to the individual making the decision. (Branch limits at CIBC, for example, range from $50,000 to $250,000, depending on the branch's location and track record.)

Types of Loans

Suppose you need money to buy a new car or renovate your home. The first step is to make certain that you don't actually have the money in some crummy investment, such as Canada Savings Bonds that return 5 per cent, as you set out to borrow at 9 per cent. If you do, you are obviously better off selling the CSBs and forgetting the loan. Of course, you will need the discipline to replace the investment if it's an essential part of your assets, such as money for your retirement.

Don't borrow from private lenders. As the federal industry department has warned, loan "brokers" who promise to find credit for individuals have a habit of pocketing an up-front fee and not arranging any credit. Never pay a fee to someone to find a loan or obtain a credit card. Don't borrow from finance companies unless your credit rating is a big problem. You're also wise never to borrow from (or lend to) friends or relatives, unless you're willing to risk alienating them (or writing off your loan).

Good relationships have a habit of turning sour when money

is involved. The natural tendency is to approach repayment in an easy-going manner, precisely because of the tie of friendship or blood. If you are hell-bent to proceed with such a loan, complete a promissory note with a fixed repayment schedule to eliminate ambiguity.

There are two types of loans: instalment and demand. Instalment loans are straightforward enough. You borrow $15,000 to buy a car and pay it back in equal instalments over a set period, usually three to five years. At a 10 per cent interest rate and a four-year term, you would pay back $380.40 a month for the 48 months. Because the payment is fixed, as your balance drops, more and more of that $380.40 goes towards paying down the $15,000 principal and less towards interest. Instalment credit is obtained for a specific purpose and has a specific repayment schedule of equal amounts. If you're able to retire the loan prematurely, it's usually worth doing so. Banks and trust companies are not allowed to apply penalties for early repayment of any loans.

A demand loan simply means the lender can "call" the loan, or demand the money back, at any time on short notice, for any reason whatsoever. Unless you (or the bank) are in big trouble, this isn't likely to happen. Demand loans have a variable and usually lower interest rate. A personal line of credit is a demand loan.

A loan can be either fixed rate or variable (or floating) rate. A three-year fixed-rate loan at 9 per cent means you agree to pay a flat 9 per cent interest charge on the outstanding balance for 36 months.

The interest rate on a variable-rate instalment loan is usually calculated at between 1 and 2 percentage points over the prime rate. At prime plus 2, if prime is 6 per cent, you will be charged 8 per cent (and if prime falls to 5.5 per cent, you will pay 7.5 per cent). Depending on your loan agreement, if rates change, either the term will be extended or shortened or your monthly payment will be adjusted, most often at the beginning of each year. Your goal should be to lessen the term, not your monthly payments. When rates are low, more of what you pay each month will go to repaying the principal; when rates are high, more will go to interest charges.

Variable-rate loans are most attractive in an environment of falling interest rates. But they are riskier, of course, since rates can easily rise in blind ignorance of your expectations and those of the experts. If you can't afford to take chances and you place a premium on "sleeping at night," the fixed-rate route – which lets you know the exact cost of the loan, over its entire life – is the way to go. An alternative is a variable-rate loan that lets you switch, without penalty, to a fixed rate, if rates go up.

Most loans are cheaper (by, say, 150 basis points or 1.5 percentage points) if they're secured. Therefore, any time you get a loan, offer whatever security you have available. A secured loan is backed by tangible assets that the bank can seize if the loan goes sour. Acceptable assets include stocks, bonds (especially Canada Savings Bonds, which have a fixed value), GICs and the cash-surrender value of your life insurance policy (though your coverage will be reduced if you use it as security). The assets cannot be held in an RRSP. You can also secure your loan with equity in your home or with other real estate. The bank will give you full value for CSBs and their own GICs and normally 50 per cent of the market value of stocks. If the stocks fall in value, the bank may well ask you to put up more security or reduce the size of your loan.

Movable assets securing a loan are called chattels. To secure a loan with chattels, you'll be required to complete a chattel mortgage (which doesn't exist in Quebec). A loan backed by real estate equity is called a collateral mortgage. An unsecured loan is backed only by your legal agreement to repay what you owe.

Car Loans

It's hardly a revelation that many people are penny wise, but pound foolish. Car buyers will trudge from car lot to car lot – just as house buyers will go from open house to open house – to get the best deal and then hurriedly arrange the financing as an afterthought. They just want the deal closed so they can drive their new vehicle off the lot. Whatever price advantage they negotiated on the purchase price can quickly be lost on the financing. Yet a vehicle is by far the largest purchase most people make, apart from their home.

A smarter approach, both for cars and mortgages (which I deal with in detail in Chapter 5), is to get approval for financing from your bank before you go shopping. You then know exactly what you can spend, which makes your decision-making easier. You know you have the funds, so you can negotiate from a position of strength. And you can then determine whether the dealer will offer you a better deal than the bank.

Consumers have a variety of financing options. Leading the list is cash. If you have it, use it. Why borrow to buy a depreciating asset, unless you have to? A few years ago I decided to buy a Mazda RX 7. I had the cash and was going to take full advantage of it. At the time, the models ranged from $20,000 for the base model to $34,000 for the fanciest model. I kept the deal simple by selling my existing car privately. Dealers really don't want trade-ins and pay poorly for them. Trade-ins do, however, allow them to mask what they are really paying you for your old car and what you are paying for your new one.

I marched into all the local dealers, waving my chequebook, and announced I was going to pay cash for a base model RX 7 within a week. I insisted I wasn't fussy about colour or options and was unwilling to negotiate them. I knew that dealers muddy deals by saying, "Listen, I'll throw in this special stereo and air

42

conditioning, worth $2,500," even when the customer doesn't really want either.

I said I would write my cheque to the dealer that gave me the best price, period. That left the dealers with the choice between making less than their normal profit or no profit at all, and seeing the buyer – who might be back in a couple of years to buy again – drive the vehicle out of a competitor's showroom. Like bankers, the last thing car salesmen want to see is a clearly committed buyer falling into the hands of the hated competition. Their first question was always, "What are you willing to pay, and what did those charlatans down at Billy Bob's Mazda say they'd sell the RX 7 to you for? I'll knock a couple of hundred bucks off their price."

Here's the secret. Don't tell them. Make it a true, blind tendering process. Force them to give you an honest, low price, out of fear they'll be beaten out. One dealer, who didn't have a base model in inventory, was so obsessed with selling that he offered to buy the model I wanted from a competitor and resell it to me at a good price! In the end, I got four blind, competitive bids and paid a bit over $19,000 for a model that, at the time, was almost never sold at a discount. I saved almost $1,000.

Your second financing choice is through the dealer. The dealer has one big advantage over your bank. You're in the showroom and Mr. or Ms. Salesperson can use financing as an inducement to buy.

Take GMAC, or General Motors Acceptance Corporation, as an example. GM's wholly owned financing arm was founded in 1919 to help dealers sell more cars and trucks. It's one of the world's biggest borrowers and lenders, financing about a third of GM vehicles. The average new vehicle contract comes in just shy of $20,000, the average term is 49 months and the average monthly payment is around $401 (about 2 per cent of vehicles are repossessed). A typical down payment is 10 per cent, but buyers must have enough cash to pay for GST and PST, which can add $3,000 to a $20,000 vehicle.

The financing arms of the auto makers generally have a tough time matching the banks on lending rates, because they lack the cheapest source of funds – depositors – and have to raise money in the money markets. Unlike banks, they have to borrow the money themselves and then re-lend it. Still, GMAC makes big bucks and contributed $1 billion (U.S.) a year to GM's bottom line even when the world's largest car maker was floundering.

To help dealers sell more vehicles, GMAC and its competitors sometimes offer incredibly low financing terms, such as 2.9 per cent, on a particular vehicle for a limited time. Does GMAC make money on this? No. How then can they afford it?

With $22 billion in sales a year in Canada, GM can afford to take a temporary hit on a model they want to move or promote. Very cheap financing is a loss leader to get you on the lot and to move slow-selling inventory. Auto manufacturers don't like this money-losing game, or the money-losing rebate game, and they are trying to get out of it. You, however, can be the beneficiary, as long as you don't have to take – or don't mind taking – a bright orange model with brown trim to get favourable financing, so that your car looks like an errant 1970s fashion statement. The dealer may give you a choice between low-rate financing and a rebate. Make sure the price hasn't quietly been jacked up to cover the easy financing or the rebate.

The financing arms of the car companies will do their best to qualify you for credit. They don't want to say no and kill the dealer's sale. GMAC is on line with Equifax, the credit bureau, and says it can give a customer an answer within 30 minutes. If your credit history is bad, they might move on to Plan B: "Maybe we could interest you in this equally good, but slightly less expensive model. It doesn't have a heater, but you can always wear your winter coat in the car." Because cars are critical to people's lives, delinquency levels are fairly low on car loans. Most people look after their mortgages first and car payments second and then juggle the rest of their obligations.

Loans from car manufacturers, which compound monthly, are structured like mortgages, with most of the interest paid early on in the term. This is called "front-end" loading, which the banks did until they were prohibited from imposing prepayment penalties under the 1980 revisions to the Bank Act. This, combined with the ravages of depreciation, means you could find yourself in an unhappy "upside-down" position, whereby your loan balance is greater than the value of the vehicle.

It's smart to make the biggest down payment you can and pay the loan back over the shortest possible term. The shorter the repayment period, the better the interest rate available. Choose a term that matches your expected ownership period. You don't want to pay out a 48-month term loan after 24 months (even though there will be no direct fees or penalties for doing so), because you will then have paid off much of the interest and mainly have principal left to repay. In other words, if you pay out your loan early, you are effectively paying a much higher interest rate than the posted rate, which is the equivalent of a prepayment penalty.

Banks are a car buyer's third option. Banks will normally lend about 80 per cent of the cost of the car. The loan is secured by the vehicle itself. Because of that and the low loan losses, the interest rate you're offered should be fairly good. If you're a member of the Canadian Automobile Association, check to see whether it has arranged any special car loan rates with banks in your area.

You might think it's impossible to beat 2.9 per cent financing from a dealer, but it isn't. A rebate and normal financing from the bank might be cheaper. You or your accountant simply have to do the math. On an $18,000 car with a $5,000 down payment, a $1,500 rebate cuts the amount to be financed to $11,500 from $13,000, and it reduces the sales tax. (That's assuming the rebate comes off the top, rather than being handed back after you pay the regular price.)

If you want to insure your car loan payments against death or disability, check first to see if you're covered by insurance you already carry. Make sure that any premiums you pay aren't added to what you borrow. Otherwise you will be paying interest on the premiums as well as the loan.

Your final option is to lease rather than buy. Now that an ordinary car can cost $20,000, more and more vehicles are being leased. Almost 40 per cent of Canadians – individuals as well as businesses – are leasing.

Leasing arrangements are extremely complex and offer absolutely no consumer protection (bank lending, by comparison, is tightly regulated). This should – and almost certainly will – change soon. Dealers encourage leasing because it allows them to turn cars over faster. If you buy, typically you will spend four years paying for the car and then hold on to it for another couple of years. In the same period you could have leased two or three vehicles.

Accountants, as unwilling to be decisive as academics, will tell you that what's best for you depends on your circumstances. Thanks, but that doesn't help. You simply have to go through the numbers, and that's not easy to do because lessors seldom tell you – and aren't required to – the real interest rate you are paying, or even the total cost. They are required to tell you only the monthly payment and the term of the lease. Get an accountant, bank or financial adviser to work out what you are really paying.

Generally speaking, leasing makes sense for some business owners, because it requires less cash flow, and for those who like to trade their car in every couple of years. (This is especially true for more expensive models.) That, however, is a costly practice, because a huge percentage of a vehicle's depreciation occurs in the first few years. Your $20,000 car will be worth $17,000 five minutes after you drive it off the lot.

Those who lease face many potential problems. You may not have been given the best price on the vehicle; you may find the lease hard to get out of early; and you may face excessive wear or mileage charges. And at the end of the term you won't own the vehicle, of course, unless you make a residual payment. Royal Bank and National Bank offer buy-back plans, which combine lower monthly payments with a guaranteed buy-back option at the end of the term.

The Automobile Protection Agency (APA), an aggressive non-profit consumer group with offices in Montreal and Toronto, can provide its members with the dealer cost of most models. They can suggest dealers or car brokers who can offer you a no-haggle price and will adhere to the APA's code of ethics.

George Iny, the Montreal-based president of the APA, says the difference between dealer cost and the manufacturer's suggested retail price (MSRP) is 7 to 8 per cent for small cars and 15 to 17 per cent on luxury cars. Dealers' margins will be less than this, because no one plays the full MSRP.

"Profits are well down," says Iny. "Customers have become very, very hard-nosed and don't believe anything they are told." Profits on options are much higher (15 to 20 per cent), which explains dealers' enthusiasm for them, and as much as 100 to 300 per cent on services such as paint sealer, fabric protector and rustproofing. Car prices are lowest in Toronto and Montreal and highest in the western provinces.

The APA also offers InfoLease, a computer program that will calculate the total cost of a lease. "Leasing is an area of substantial abuse, misrepresentation and public ignorance," says Iny.

Robert Lo Presti, who used to work for the APA, has developed a program called CarCalculator, which will compute the relative advantages of leasing and borrowing, with or without a rebate. It's available for $29.95 from Orangesoft, Box 33518, 1277 York Mills Rd., North York, Ontario, M3A 1Z5. *The Canadian Red Book*, published by Maclean Hunter and available from libraries, lists prices of used cars.

RRSP Loans

These loans are good for you, and good for your bank. Most financial institutions market them heavily during the January and February RRSP season, offering them at prime. If you're a favoured client, you may even get a better rate – just remember to ask, because your branch sure won't suggest it to you.

Most institutions make RRSP loans at prime provided that you use the funds to buy a product offered by them or their brokerage subsidiary. For example, you can use a Commerce Bank RRSP loan for products of the bank or its broker, Wood Gundy. Some institutions, such as TD, will even lend you the money and let you use it to buy a competitor's products. Amazing, but true.

A second typical condition is that the RRSP loan must be repaid within a year, which is also good for you and good for your bank. RRSP customers, who by definition are preparing for their retirement, are the kind banks love to attract, so the loans are made to stop them from shopping elsewhere. Because of the tax-free status of RRSPs, it's usually worthwhile to borrow the money. The interest paid on RRSP loans, however, is not tax deductible and hasn't been since 1981.

Other Investment Loans

If you want to borrow to buy stocks or bonds, the first place to look is your brokerage firm. It will offer loans at great rates, often below prime. Though you can use the money for any purpose, the brokerage realizes that chances are you will use it to buy more stocks or bonds and generate commission dollars for the firm.

If you have a "margin" account, you can borrow 50 cents on the dollar against most stocks you hold, and more on bonds. (Many people think "margin" is the money the broker puts up. Wrong. It's what *you* put up.) In other words, if you have Imperial Oil shares with a market value of $20,000, the broker will lend you $10,000. The government won't allow you to buy on margin within an RRSP, on the grounds that you shouldn't be putting your retirement money at risk.

There are two problems with buying on margin. Problem one. You borrow at 7 per cent and your stock ends up returning 3 per cent, so you suffer a net loss. It's actually worse than this example suggests, because you must compare the after-tax returns on your investment with the interest you pay. If your marginal tax rate is 50 per cent and you are borrowing money at 8 per cent, you need a return of 16 per cent on any fully taxed investment just to come out even (capital gains and dividends are not fully taxed). How likely is that?

Problem two. Your portfolio hits the skids and you get a margin call – that is, your broker phones you in a panic and demands you put up more money *tout de suite*. The shares you have offered as security are now worth less than double the amount borrowed. Hillary Rodham Clinton gave up her lucrative commodity trading in the late 1970s, you'll recall, after she received a margin call and got cold feet.

The appeal of borrowing to buy stocks or bonds is the leverage it provides. You put up relatively little to own a lot, which is great when prices are going up, and less than great when they're not. Leverage accelerates gains – but does the same thing to losses. And borrowing to buy securities that pay interest or dividends (or have the potential to pay dividends, meaning all common stocks) is tax deductible. You normally lose that deductibility when you sell your investment, unless you re-invest the proceeds in another qualifying investment. Banks will often lend you money at favourable rates to buy investments, as long as the purpose of the loan is something more thought out than, "I'd like the money to try to corner the world silver market, just like those fun-loving Hunt brothers did in 1980."

Borrow for investment purposes rather than for personal needs, so that you can take advantage of the tax break. Pay off non-deductible loans before deductible ones. Keep good records of investment loans, so you can easily prove their purpose to Revenue Canada.

Personal Lines of Credit (PLCs)

"You'll feel more comfortable with money behind you," suggests the Scotiabank PLC ad, showing – with a wonderful touch for the literal – a cushion (perhaps full of money) labelled Scotia Line, sitting on an arm chair under a soft light.

Get a PLC if you possibly can. It's the Rolls-Royce of lending, and a growth category. You will need a good credit record and a personal income in the range of $35,000 or, for a joint line, a household income of $50,000. Secured credit lines are available for as much as $150,000.

If you set up a line for $10,000 you can use that money any way, any time you like. You simply write cheques for whatever amount you want. In most cases, you need never see your banker again, or go into the branch on bended knee with some improbable, convoluted story about why you absolutely have to have

cash within 24 hours. As long as you make your monthly payments, you can write cheques and be a wastrel, and your bank
will be none the wiser.

Your cheques on your PLC could be the cheapest and easiest
way to finance your renos or pay off higher interest debts. It isn't
the best way to finance a depreciating asset like a car, which you
want to pay off quickly with a fixed-term instalment loan. If you
use a line of credit to contribute to an RRSP at the bank, you
could be eligible for bonus interest. Because a line of credit can
be used for a variety of purposes, it's particularly useful to those
who are financially active.

PLCs offer revolving credit, like credit cards, but on far better
terms. They have no fixed term and are usually variable rate.
Unlike many loans, they allow you to borrow exactly what you
need, so you don't pay interest on funds not yet required. For
example, you can write cheques to pay for your renos as your
project proceeds. The bank will offer you a better rate than for
almost any other loan, particularly if the line is secured. A good
customer who uses a home as security could pay as little as half a
point above prime.

For most PLCs, you pay back 3 per cent of the outstanding balance every month, or a minimum of $50. You can repay as much
as you want at any time without penalty.

In short, the interest rate on a PLC is favourable, the hassle
minimal, and if you have one in place before something awful –
such as being laid off – happens to you, you will have a ready
source of funds when you most need it, without having to
approach your banker.

Bankers say that a lot of lines of credit go unused. For many
people, however, there's a tendency to use credit if they have it
and to treat a PLC as a chequing account instead of as a loan facility – and facility is certainly the right word. It's easy to run PLCs up

towards their limits, not for major purchases but simply as a matter of course. People who do that are living beyond their means, with the bank's tacit blessing. They would never have borrowed the money if they had had to go into the bank to arrange a loan, particularly if it's for day-to-day purposes. Remember that you are borrowing money when you write cheques on your line of credit.

Consolidation Loans

There are good and bad consolidation loans. The better ones bring order out of chaos in your financial affairs. You might, for example, take three small, older high-interest loans and renegotiate them into one larger, lower interest loan. This obviously can be done most easily in an environment of low or falling interest rates. You save money and make life easier for yourself. One strategy is to make the same monthly payment that you did before, and get yourself out of debt faster.

Bad consolidation loans are taken out by those who are suffering under a burden of debts and are desperate to reduce their monthly payments. If you find yourself in that position, talk to your banker sooner rather than later, before your credit rating has taken a dive. The total monthly payment on one $10,000 loan will likely be less than the payments on five $2,000 loans, and easier to keep track of. If one or more of those loans is on your credit cards, a consolidation loan will certainly be cheaper.

Before making any decision, compare the terms (and total monthly payments) of a consolidation loan with those of the loans you are presently paying. A consolidation loan will ultimately do you no good if it simply allows you to delay coming to terms with poor credit practices.

Be forewarned that some banks are leery of such loans. They know that you could simply be asking them to exchange a *small* high-risk loan (or loans) for a *large* high-risk loan. The minimum loan could be $10,000, and you will have to provide security for it.

Reno Loans

Renovations can be financed in a variety of ways, depending on the cost and the period over which you will need the money. Smaller projects can be paid for by using a regular line of credit or a home improvement loan.

Those planning bigger expenditures should consider a Home Equity Loan or Home Equity Line of Credit. These can also be used for other big expenditures, such as the purchase of property or investments. They allow you to take advantage of the equity you have built up in your home to get access to low-cost, long-term credit, with repayment amortized over as much as 25 years. The bank will lend you up to 75 per cent of the appraised value of your home, less outstanding mortgages. If your house is worth $200,000 and you have a $125,000 mortgage, you can borrow .75 x $200,000 = $150,000, minus $125,000 = $25,000. You will have to pay for an assessment of your home and the costs of a collateral mortgage, which should be similar to those for a first mortgage.

A Home Equity Line of Credit has all the advantages of any other line of credit. Because the limit will be much higher, you may be able to choose between repaying both principal and interest (say 2 per cent per month, or a $100 minimum), and interest only.

Other options to finance a renovation include remortgaging your property to the level normally acceptable for a first mortgage, or "adding on" to an existing mortgage.

Banks like renovation loans if the reno clearly adds value to your property. They would rather lend to have you modernize your kitchen or bathroom, the two most important rooms when a house is put up for sale, than to install a swimming pool, which can actually drive purchasers away. Pools require a lot of maintenance, can be dangerous, are useless to those who don't like swimming, and take up most of a backyard and garden space.

Student Loans

Student loans are notorious for their high delinquency rate. Twenty per cent of borrowers do not repay Canada Student Loans in full and on time; 13 per cent do so only after debt collectors are sent after them, or the government recovers the money owed out of income tax refunds; 7 per cent default. It's hard to believe any institution would want to finance these loans, but Ottawa has put them up for grabs and interested a couple of the banks in taking them over.

CIBC has aggressively been acquiring the rights to provincial student loan programs. In the case of Alberta, for example, the bank took over the loans in return for a 5 per cent "risk premium" from the government to help cover losses.

The high delinquency rate on the loans is presumably the result of students' resentment at paying for their education, and the fact that they are given out on the basis of need rather than creditworthiness. In any event, many students who sob over Spinoza and quarrel over quarks are apparently above paying their debts. They could change their mind if the banks begin reporting student loans to the credit bureau, as CIBC is thinking of doing.

Students scouting for bucks should begin their search by checking to see what bursaries and scholarships their college or university offers. Many summers ago, I was doing the usual student-discovers-self (and much else) in Europe, when I received my undergraduate marks. They looked pretty good, so I wrote to the university awards department and asked if I qualified for anything. To my astonishment, a few weeks later I was informed that I had been awarded two scholarships, with cheques to follow.

Students who need to borrow should start by inquiring at the student financial aid office of their institution or province. The government offers one-stop shopping, with the province or territory determining needs and eligibility both for provincial programs and for the 30-year-old Canada Student Loans Program (Quebec and the Northwest Territories have opted out and have their own programs). The province issues a certificate to those who are eligible, which the borrower takes to a lender.

The average value of Canada Student Loans negotiated by full-time students in 1992-93 was $2,994; by part-time students, $1,991. In recent years, more women than men have received loans. About 57 per cent of students have a total indebtedness to the program of less than $5,000; 28 per cent owe $5,000 to $10,000; the remaining 15 per cent owe more than $10,000.

Just remember what will become all too obvious the day you graduate. You have to pay borrowed money back and it's something less than an unalloyed joy to do so, as you are starting out on a career. Even though repayment can be deferred in distress cases, you don't even want to think of the possibility of having no job and massive student loans to repay.

Repayment can be stretched out over as much as nine-and-a-half years, but it's smart to repay a student loan as quickly as you can. (In my own case, however, the interest rate payable on the loan was far below the deposit rate, so I had little incentive to pay off the balance.)

Keep in touch with your lender if you are having difficulties or if you move. If you don't, you could discover the alacrity with which the government pursues its wayward student loan borrowers. "The banks get out cleanly, but the government then sics the collection agencies on these people, and they run them to ground," says Gerard Kennedy, executive director of Toronto's Daily Bread Food Bank, some of whose users have been affected. "It's unbelievable what goes on."

The banks have their own separate offerings, which you can

consider if you're not eligible for government assistance or need supplemental financing. The Bank of Montreal, in a wonderfully insulting ad, asks, "Is your bank account emptier than your head at the start of an exam?" Or, they might have asked, emptier than the average copywriter's brain?

Banks generally offer students favourable terms, because they want to line you up early as a lifetime customer. Under the Bank of Montreal's program, you pay only interest on your loan for the period you're in school and have seven years after graduation to repay the full amount. This lifetime customer ploy often backfires, however, since many students eternally resent the bank that lends them the money and then hounds them for repayment.

Overdraft Protection

Overdraft protection can be useful, as long as it's not abused. As it turns out, I was an abuser. I recently got this warm, personal letter from my branch's loans manager:

"Dear Customer: We are pleased to see that you have found your personal Credit Reserve useful in meeting your temporary credit line which is to revolve on a regular basis. As of June 20, our records indicate your Credit Reserve is not operating in this manner due to the following condition:

"Continuing overdraft position for 6 months without cover in full.

"...I would ask that you make arrangements to correct the above condition immediately."

So shoot me. The money was available, so I spent it.

Overdraft protection is no substitute for a PLC or a proper loan. It's expensive. You could pay a fee of a bit over a buck a month and very high interest rates on whatever overdraft you have. But having the protection will allow you to avoid the cost, embarrassment and inconvenience of NSF cheques. They can cost as much as $20 a bounce, double the rate of the mid-1980s. (Bankers say the steep penalty is meant to serve as a deterrent. Numbers aren't available in Canada, but in the United States last year, banks collected $4.35 billion [U.S.] in fees for bounced cheques, of which $3.67 billion was profit).

Get overdraft protection, but at the same time keep better track of your cash flow so you don't have to use it. A typical offering is CIBC's aptly named COPS, for CIBC Overdraft Protection Service. It has limits of from $200 to $5,000 and stipulates that your account must have a positive balance for at least one day a month.

How to Get What You Want

You want a loan, but you don't want to dig yourself into credit hell? Here are some tips.

• Don't borrow more than you absolutely need, particularly when you are young and starting out, or when you are nearing retirement and the end of certain cash flow. It's easy to forget it's borrowed money you're spending, money you will have to repay, with interest, in after-tax dollars. Remember that at a 50 per cent marginal tax rate, the 8 per cent you are paying on your loan is the equivalent of earning 16 per cent in after-tax dollars.

• Shop around. Don't limit your travels to the big banks. "If you have a loan with one of the banks, you're probably paying too much interest. We can easily transfer your bank loan to our low rate SuperLoan," says Canada Trust. Wave the ad in their face and challenge them to better what the bank offers.

You'll do better by forgetting the 1-800 number and going into a branch, particularly if you're known there, or your credit record is shaky. Phone applicants are judged entirely on credit scoring. If you go in, you will have the chance to explain – apologize for? – your less than perfect record, and the loans officer will see face to face what a fine human being you are. Your chances will go up.

• Be prepared. Be confident. Don't let the process intimidate you. Know exactly what you owe and own, and be prepared to explain clearly why you need the money. Phone ahead for an appointment and ask what information and documents you will need. Be ready to answer questions, to impress the banker favourably and to save him or her time.

• Be honest with the bank. Every banker I interviewed said dishonesty is the fastest way to ensure your application is declined. Don't forget that the bank will be able to check virtually everything you tell them anyway. So if there are some obvious holes in your credit history, be the first to tell them, and explain the circumstances.

• Be honest with yourself. Maybe you do have a credit or spending problem. Maybe your in-laws are right and you are a bit of a deadbeat about paying your bills. Or maybe the bank is right: you don't really need, and can't afford, a new sports car on your $35,000-a-year salary.

A decade ago, when I was a more brazen investor than I am now, I tried to borrow money because I *knew* the price of gold bullion was going up and I wanted to take advantage of it. The loan idea was a bad one, though I foolishly didn't appreciate the loans officer telling me just that. I didn't get the loan. Instant karma – gold went down.

• If your credit is good, you should be able to get exactly what you want. Worry less about getting your loan quickly – borrow in haste, repent at leisure – and more about getting the terms that suit you. Remind the loans officer that the banks use the phrase "custom tailor" in their ads. Specifically, here's what to ask about:

• *First,* interest rates: If the rate is what you care most about, and your credit record is good, you can get banks to compete for your business. If it's a big loan, ask for a half point off the posted rate; try for a quarter point if the loan is smaller.

CIBC's Pat Skene says her bank gives the branches guidelines, but the managers have full discretion to match the competition for good customers. "Branch managers can use discretion, to whatever [extent] they choose, to price that loan to match the competition, to keep that relationship with CIBC."

The key to borrowing is to know exactly what you will be paying in interest and fees, if any, and what you will have to shell out monthly. Can you really afford on your miserable salary to come up with $600 a month for new car payments? Will it make life easier if you swallow hard and buy a less pretentious car, or even a used one, and pay only $450?

Don't let the bank snow you. The prime lending rate is the base rate the banks charge their most creditworthy customers, mostly big corporations. But some banks now use something called the "consumer prime rate" or the "consumer base rate." It's usually higher than the prime rate. In November 1992, National Trust wrote to me and to other holders of their To-talLine line of credit to inform us that the interest rate would no longer be based on the prime rate, but on something called the TotalLine Base Rate.

• *Second,* term: Negotiate the shortest repayment period you can, given your cash flow, to reduce interest charges. This is particularly important on loans to acquire depreciating assets, such as cars. One bank advertises a car loan that can be repaid for up to seven years, by which time most cars are worth about 50 cents.

• *Third,* repayment schedule: You should be able to arrange to repay the loan at intervals that best match your cash flow, whether weekly, biweekly or monthly. You will repay your loan more quickly, of course, if you repay $100 a week rather than $400 a month, because over a year you will repay $5,200 rather than $4,800.

• *Fourth,* repayment options: Try to avoid repaying interest only, an option that may be available on secured loans or PLCs. Otherwise, you will still be repaying the loan as they whisk you around the nursing home with a blanket over your lap. By definition, an interest-only loan is never repaid.

• *Fifth,* loan size: The bank's perfect customer will have a great credit record and want to borrow a lot of money for a good reason. But many customers want to borrow only a small amount, say, under $5,000. The bank will make next to nothing on the loan because the cost of the time spent with the customer and the administration cost ($60 an hour full costed, according to one source) will eat up much of the profit. You will pay a higher rate for a small loan than for a large one, because the fixed costs are a larger percentage of the loan.

Your chances of getting a small amount are better if (i) you are already a good customer of the branch or (ii) you are a brand-new customer who might move your other bank business to that branch. Customers with a personal line of credit circumvent the problem by simply writing themselves a cheque.

• *Sixth,* fine print: Be a Philadelphia lawyer. Read the fine print of whatever loan document is shoved under your nose, and ask for a full explanation of any points you don't understand. Never sign a blank sheet.

• If you can't afford to take chances, or you sleep better at night knowing all the bases are covered, look at the loan insurance your bank offers. Most have life insurance, disability insurance and insurance to cover job loss. Compare that with whatever your insurance company can offer.

Remember that few investments can match the real returns of debt reduction. Try to repay your loan more quickly than the agreement requires.

• If your total debt service ratio (discussed in Chapter 5) is high, you can either borrow less or extend the term of the repayments to keep the ratio acceptable. Of course, by paying over a longer period you will pay more interest.

What to Do If You Are Turned Down

"People don't understand if they get turned down for a loan. Complaints about that are taken incredibly seriously, and very often we reverse decisions that are made at the branches," says TD's Stephen Stewart. "A letter to the president can be very, very effective. The least you will get is a reasonable, or maybe a clearer, explanation of why you were turned down. It doesn't cost them anything to pick up the phone and say, I have a problem ... If they don't tell us, we will never know. Somebody out there could be making a lot of really lousy decisions."

There are many reasons why credit applications are turned down. The applicant could have a bad credit history, not be in a position to repay the loan easily, be a frequent "credit seeker," have too much credit available already, or have provided inaccurate or misleading information to the lender. Refusal rates for loans and credit cards are between 20 per cent and 40 per cent, depending on the institution.

If you are refused, don't give up. The first thing to do, after sobbing hysterically and letting the air out of the bank manager's tires, is to find out what went wrong. At least two people will have seen the application before it is refused. Ask why you were turned down. In the United States, but not here, financial institutions are obliged to tell you. The bankers I interviewed were unanimous that you have a right to know why they said *nyet*. They don't want to send away an existing or potential customer in a huff.

Ask yourself again if your loan proposal makes sense, and if you really do need the money. Should you try again? Or should you simply give up?

If you conclude that yes, you need the money, and yes, your proposal makes sense, move on to Plan B. Ask your banker what you can do to make the proposal acceptable. Make arrangements for a co-signer? Put up more security? Ask for a loan for a Honda Civic rather than a Nissan 300 ZX? Limit your renovation plans? If, however, you don't want to cut back on the size of your loan, try taking your proposal to a different lender.

The final option is simply to wait. If you are intent on buying that 300 ZX, strengthen your credibility and your financial position by depositing $600 a month for six months in an account, which is what you would pay on your car loan. Return to the prospective lender and impress him or her with your discipline, not to mention the larger down payment you've accumulated, and ask to be reconsidered.

A word of warning. Bankers are cagey, and they have excellent access to information. If you apply for a loan and the bank then checks with the credit bureau, that fact will appear on your credit file. If you're turned down by Banker A and go down the street to Banker B, the latter will know about your application and will undoubtedly be curious why it didn't pan out. It's like two-timing – sooner or later it catches up to you.

Minority Lending

Lending to minorities is not a big issue in Canada, at least not yet. But the country's ethnic makeup is changing radically with each passing day, as anyone walking down the street in Toronto, Montreal, or Vancouver can see in seconds. Minority lending is a huge issue in the United States, discussed at length on almost a daily basis in the press.

Under the 1977 Community Reinvestment Act, American financial institutions are required to lend wherever they take deposits. The problem is that in many inner-city neighbourhoods, with their heavy concentrations of blacks and Hispanics, those institutions are more adept at taking money out than at putting it back in.

A *Wall Street Journal* study of more than 3 million mortgage applications found that the denial rate was 34 per cent for blacks and 17 per cent for whites. Even blacks making $100,000 (U.S.) a year or more faced almost double the rejection rate of comparable whites. Awarding and denying credit on the basis of race or religion is against the law in the United States, as it is in Canada.

Under the Clinton administration, the issue has moved to the front burner. Government regulators even blocked a bank takeover by Boston-based Shawmut National Corp. because it had practised discriminatory lending. A few banks that were shamed or pressured into lending to minorities and low-income people have been pleasantly surprised by the results. Mellon Bank has begun to provide financial counselling and mortgages to people in those groups in Philadelphia and discovered that the loans entail fewer losses than anticipated, can be profitable, and expand the bank's customer base. Low-income people don't want to lose their homes, once given the chance to own them. Many of them pay less for their mortgages than they did for rent.[1]

This issue has yet to hit the front pages in Canada, though at least one bank has looked at how to deal with immigrants who don't meet the usual criteria – or can't prove their creditworthiness with documents – but are still good risks. For example, the bank might begin including rent from boarders as part of income, knowing that that is a common source of income for many newly arrived families. The banks aren't doing this out of the goodness of their hearts, though they should be given credit for it. Rather, they see a new, unexploited customer base.

Of course the banks are falling over themselves to lend to at least some aboriginal groups. While many native people live in poverty, some do not. They have grown wealthy as a result of resources, particularly oil, or land claims settlements. The lending is not only good public relations, it's good business. The Bank of Montreal has appointed a Mohawk from the Six Nations Reserve near Brantford, Ontario, as vice-president of aboriginal banking. In a well-publicized ceremony in October 1993, at its Toronto headquarters, the bank signed an agreement to lend $88 million to Inuvialuit Regional Corp. of Inuvik (the Inuit are the largest holders of mineral rights in the country). Let's hope they keep it up.

Mostafa Moshtaghi is an immigrant from Iran, with a Master's degree from an American college, who works as a youth employment counsellor in Toronto. He described for me some of the credit problems new Canadians face. Many new arrivals don't speak the language well and don't have collateral or credit histories. Many have no idea how a system that relies on credit works. In many Third World countries, credit cards are unknown, except among a wealthy minority, and lending depends much more on personal relationships than on business.

"You have to prove to banks that you don't need the money before they'll lend it to you," says Moshtaghi, uttering a familiar refrain. He says that banks in areas such as Parkdale, a poorer area of Toronto, will accept welfare cheques as deposits but will not lend to those depositors.

Moshtaghi's solution has been to set up an informal Community Trust that allows its contributors – friends and acquaintances who can't get credit – to borrow money interest-free from a pool, according to need and on the basis of trust. It's better, he says, than paying 15 per cent to Household Finance or to a loan broker, who will take a fat up-front fee "to lie for you" to a lender.

Meanwhile, the Toronto-based Black Business and Professional Association, which believes the banks discriminate against black business people – a charge the banks deny – wants to increase the number of branches (from one) of the Caribbean Canadian African (Ontario) Credit Union, of which it is a major shareholder.

Gerard Kennedy, executive director of Toronto's Daily Bread Food Bank, the largest food bank in North America, says its users often face an unfriendly reception from the banks, even though food recipients have on average worked six years and three months, and many have a long relationship with a bank. Many banks refuse to let low-income people open an account – an estimated 50,000 of them a year in the Toronto area – most often because they lack sufficient ID or enough money to meet the minimum balance requirement.

Many also refuse to cash welfare cheques – even when they know the individual – or do so only after holding the cheque for 10 days or longer, which is tough for low-income people. The banks bid in various parts of the country for the contract to cash the cheques, in return for a government guarantee. They are worried about fraud, even though a Quebec government study showed that only 0.04 per cent of welfare cheques are cashed fraudulently, and the federal government reimburses institutions for such transactions to a maximum of $1,500 per cheque.[2] Many food bank users are forced to turn to cheque-cashing outlets, which charge outrageous fees. The Daily Bread Food Bank helped to persuade some outlets to lower their fee for cashing welfare cheques to 2.9 per cent from 4.9 per cent.

"I've taken homeless people into banks and tried to get their cheques cashed, and had to indemnify myself," says Kennedy. He describes the plight of Gary – whom I knew when I was a volunteer – a homeless man with a mental age of twelve. As a child, Gary was confined with a dog to the attic of an abusive foster home, rather than sent to school. Because the bank wouldn't give him a card with which to deposit and withdraw money – originally, it wouldn't even give him an account – he had to carry what money he had with him and was constantly being robbed. The bank in question is the bank of Daily Bread, which has a large sum on deposit. "I think the bank's action was entirely arbitrary," says Kennedy. "What other customer gets turned down?"

"It's just discrimination against those who don't look reliable," he continues. "Once they're on welfare, they start getting treated differently. It starts with not being able to cash your cheque. It's not smart business. All but a few of these people are eventually going to get back on their feet."

Summary
• Don't be intimidated when you go in to a branch to arrange a loan. Remember that if your credit is good, the bank needs and wants your business.
• Your position will be stronger if you or your family already have a lot of business with the bank. Don't hesitate to ask for a preferred lending rate.
• Don't borrow from loan brokers. Never pay a fee to someone to find a loan. Don't borrow from (or lend to) friends or relatives.
• Don't borrow more than you need.
• Shop around.
• Your chances of getting credit are greater in person than over the phone.
• Know your financial situation and be prepared to explain exactly why you need a loan.
• Be honest when you apply.
• Read the loan documents carefully before signing them. Ask questions.
• If you are turned down, ask why. Don't give up.
• Don't borrow to buy a depreciating asset unless you have to. Keep the repayment term short.
• Don't treat the financing of your car purchase as an after-

thought.

• Be aware of the risks involved in buying securities "on margin."

• RRSP loans are a good idea, if they are repaid quickly.

• Consider getting a personal line of credit, even if you don't need it now.

• Get overdraft protection rather than writing NSF cheques.

• Repay non-tax-deductible debts with the highest interest rate first – even before your mortgage.

I have one credit card.
Why do I need any more?

DOUGLAS GOOLD TO DAVID LIVINGSTON,
SENIOR VICE-PRESIDENT, VISA, TD BANK

You don't. There's no reason
why people need more than one card ...
The only reason people do, typically,
is that the limits are not high enough.
It's kind of a Catch-22.
The limits aren't high enough
because you have more than one card.

DAVID LIVINGSTON

CHAPTER 3

PLASTIC EXPLOSIVES AND HOW TO HANDLE THEM

The Card Business in Canada

Most Canadians know that charges on credit cards are outrageous, but that doesn't stop them from dishing out millions every year in fees and interest payments. Ironically, they could easily minimize these charges and, with discipline, avoid them entirely. That's becoming even easier now that the card market is saturated. Issuers have become noticeably more competitive, thanks to the slower economy of the 90s, widespread concern about high personal debt levels, and the aging of the baby boomers.

For years, card issuers kept rates at dizzying levels, despite falling rates for other forms of credit, with Visa establishing a record for bank cards in November 1991 by charging 12 percentage points over the bank rate. Retail cards were long ago frozen at 28.8 per cent – a rate which applied even when the prime rate was 5.75 per cent. Some card issuers have been forced, however, to lower rates on at least some cards to maintain market share. Others have taken a different tack and tried to entice consumers by offering them a bewildering array of benefits, ranging from grandfather clocks to points towards free flights. In many cases, these are "benefits" that card holders don't want or need and would never consider – or probably even think of – were they not marketed so aggressively.

Even though the real explosion in the use of plastic is behind us, Canadians still hold 25 million Visa and MasterCard bank cards, the equivalent of almost one per person – babies included. This is one of the highest levels in the world. The number of cards in circulation balloons to 55 million if you include all types of credit or charge cards. About 30 per cent of Canadians don't have a bank card, either because they don't want one or don't qualify for one. Visa and MasterCard are now used for almost $50 billion worth of transactions a year, quadruple the level of a decade ago, with an average sale of $67. However, the number that is most disturbing, because it reflects the money wasted on cards – overwhelmingly the most expensive form of debt – is the outstanding balance on the two cards. That stands at an eye-popping $11.4 billion, which suggests that Canadians pay billions more in interest charges to the banks than they need to.

Of course card issuers not only collect fees and interest charges from consumers, they also collect fees (the "discount" or "interchange") of from 1.5 to 4 per cent from merchants that accept their cards. When you put a $100 purchase on your card, the retailer has to pay the financial institution with which it has an agreement between $1.50 and $4.00 (which the institution splits with the bank or trust named on the card, if the two are different). Much of the profit of big American banks like Citibank comes from credit cards. Despite similar advantages, Canada's financial institutions claim that for years they lost money on their card operations, pointing to steep administrative costs and high write-offs.

The 1991 testimony of the major banks, Canada Trust and American Express before the House of Commons Consumer and Corporate Affairs committee – the third parliamentary committee to study credit cards in the last half dozen years – is full of complaints about the lack of profitability of card operations, though all the witnesses resolutely refused to reveal their specific profit and loss figures.

"It took us 14 years to break even on our business venture of starting the MasterCard brand," Alan McNally, vice-chairman of Bank of Montreal, told the committee. "This is a narrow margin business." Brent Kelman, an executive vice-president at Canada Trust, added, "I can tell you if we were to accumulate the profits and losses in those 13 years [of issuing MasterCards] at this point, we'd be in a net loss position." As an exasperated witness for the Consumers' Association of Canada commented, Canada's financial institutions "may be world-class, and all that, but if they can't make money when prime is at 8 per cent and credit card rates are at 20 per cent, then they shouldn't be in the business. You can't slice it both ways." [1]

The card business is now profitable, but the banks won't say just how profitable. Most issuers are using those profits not to cut the rate on cards aggressively, but to lower fees and add benefits in the struggle to increase market share. CIBC's senior vice-president for card products, Paul Vessey, said in an interview that Canadian issuers don't make what their American counterparts do, but added, "I think to sit down and say this is a business where we want to make between 15 and 25 per cent return on equity is probably an accurate number."

Types of Cards

Bank cards

Visa, originally BankAmericard in the United States, began life in Canada in 1968 as Chargex. On launch day, Chargex hired five women to drive Camaros with blue, white and gold racing stripes around Toronto to iron out any problems that merchants had with the cards.[2] Its main competitor, Master Charge, crossed the border in 1973, becoming MasterCard in 1980 (by then, the word "charge" had unpleasant connotations). Visa and MasterCard are bank cards, issued by financial institutions including banks, trust companies, credit unions and *caisses populaires*. They are the most prevalent cards and will be the focus of our discussion, though most of what we say about them also applies to other cards.

The Royal Bank of Canada is the country's largest issuer of Visa cards, with 4.4 million in circulation, while the Bank of Montreal is the biggest issuer of MasterCard, with more than 4 million cards. Each financial institution (not the parent organizations, Visa International and MasterCard International) sets its own rates and terms for its cards. The non-profit parent associations serve as franchisers for the thousands of financial institutions around the world that make up their memberships. Unlike American Express, which is part of the Dow Jones industrial average on the New York Stock Exchange, they are not public companies and hence do not have shares that trade on an exchange.

The defining characteristic of bank cards is that they offer revolving credit. That means that while the cardholder has to make a minimum payment each due date, usually 3 to 5 per cent of the outstanding balance, the remainder can be carried forward indefinitely as a cumulative balance. This, needless to say, is the Achilles heel of the cards for many consumers. By comparison, with instalment credit, the usual form of credit for personal loans, the borrower has to make a fixed repayment, usually monthly, according to a schedule agreed upon at the time of the loan.

Visa and MasterCard have preset credit limits, usually $1,000 or more for regular cards and $5,000 or more for premium cards. There is no interest charged on goods and services purchased from merchants when the balance is paid in full within the grace period, which is usually 21 days. Cash advances are available through automated teller or banking machines, with interest starting from the receipt of the loan. Annual fees range from zero, for some MasterCards, to $175 for the more expensive of

TD's two gold Visa cards. (We will ignore platinum cards, which only a handful of cardholders carry and which offer little of value beyond snob appeal.)

Entertainment and travel cards

American Express would like to pretend it's a bank, having persuaded former prime minister Brian Mulroney, amidst huge controversy, to allow it to establish the Amex Bank of Canada in 1988. Of course, it's a bank with no depositors and none of the services that the country's other chartered banks offer. The American Express card is an entertainment and travel charge card, like Diners Club (Diners is "immensely prestigious internationally," say the ads) and enRoute, which have been merged recently by their new owner, Citibank Canada.

Charge card balances must be paid off in full by the due date each month. Amex's delinquency fees kick in if a charge is not paid in full by the date of your next billing statement, at a 30 per cent nominal annual rate. As with other financial delinquencies, if you get referred to a collection agency, you have to pay their costs, too. American Express introduced its Optima card in 1988 to compete against the bank cards; it operates exactly as they do, while offering different interest rate levels for different levels of creditworthiness.

American Express sells itself by claiming superior service, through clever "lifestyle" advertisements that appeal to people's insecurities and pretensions. Consumers are seductively invited to become "members" of an exclusive cardholders' "club," a brash claim indeed, considering that the club has 34 million members, which is far greater than the entire population of Canada (and considering that American Express recently concluded a card agreement with not-so-exclusive K mart). Amex ads have featured the hip and famous – including Ella Fitzgerald and Quincy Jones,

blacks who 30 years ago would not have been served in many of
the establishments bearing the Amex logo, as journalist Anne
Kingston has wryly observed. Now we are to led to believe, she
adds, that the colour that segregates is the colour of your credit
card.[3]

Through its advertisements, American Express tells its members that they have "no preset spending limit," the implication
being that they can spend to their hearts' content on their plastic. As cardholders who have spent beyond their usual level soon
find out, this is not the case – Amex quickly contacts them for an
explanation.

Amex's market share has been eroding for years, the legacy of
corporate infighting, high merchant and consumer fees, and the
company's notorious arrogance, which has made it slow to combine with other corporate names to offer "co-branded" cards.

Retail and gasoline cards

These cards are offered by retailers such as Sears or by oil companies such as Petro-Canada to increase customer loyalty and are
valid only at the issuer's place of business. The cards offer discounts
on some of their products as well as Air Miles, Club Z points, and
so on. The retail cards are a suicide form of plastic unless paid off
every month, since they have always had ferociously high interest
rates, even as other market rates plunged. Balances, however, are
much lower than on other cards. Except for Petro-Canada, the oil
cards are charge cards on which no balance is supposed to be carried, with late penalty rates of 24 or so per cent.

The nominal annual rate you are quoted is calculated monthly. This was the key issue during a recent, unsuccessful appeal
supported by a consumer advocacy group to the Supreme Court
of Canada. That means a nominal annual rate of 28.8 per cent is
calculated as 2.4 per cent a month, which when compounded

gives you an effective annual rate of 32.9 per cent (though no one would ever pay it, because no retailer would allow a cardholder to go a year without payment). These cards also charge interest on interest, which means you will pay interest this month on last month's already steep, unpaid interest bill.

The retail and gas cards do have advantages: they have no fees, give greater credit for partial payments (as explained below), and have longer grace periods than bank cards. Though all the big retailers now accept bank cards, they prefer customers to use their own cards, particularly so they don't have to ante up fees to the banks.

Debit cards

These cards are becoming available across the country. Though they have met with some resistance south of the border, where a Visa official has admitted the word "debit" is unhappily close to the word "debt," the banks say they are pleased with their early reception here. Because our chequing system is one of the world's most efficient and fast, Canadians – unlike Americans – are not used to playing the "float game," taking advantage of the days it takes to clear a cheque. They are therefore likely to view a debit card as an electronic cheque.

Consumers use their regular bank card and personal identification number (PIN) to pay for purchases at designated outlets, notably supermarkets and grocery stores, through a direct debit or draw-down on a bank account. The banks love debit cards because they represent a cheaper, cashless way of doing business, eliminate the problem of bouncing cheques and – unlike credit cards – earn a return on every transaction from both the merchant and the consumer. The cards also reveal consumers' spending habits, information that is useful for target marketing.

The cards are more convenient than cheques, and users know

they are spending what they have and no more (unless they are attached to overdraft protection or lines of credit). However, they're hit with a charge of 30 to 60 cents a transaction, depending on which financial institution's card they use. Debit cards, however, lack the best feature of credit cards, which is free credit during the grace period and – for some at least – no transaction fee. They are also yet another inducement to spend more. "People who pay with their banking card tend to purchase more than when they pay cash," says a CIBC brochure for retailers.

Consumers should consider (i) how much they are willing to pay for convenience, (ii) how useful it is to have a card that may make overspending more difficult and (iii) what it costs them to write a cheque instead of using the debit card. Costs for either or both may be less if consumers maintain a minimum monthly balance in their account, or if they have a fee package from their bank. (Fee packages are discussed later.)

Based on the American experience and the early indications in Canada, the banks think the cards will largely replace cheques and cash, which together still account for 85 per cent of transactions. They predict their growth will be huge. "It's taken us 25 years to do the level of transaction volume we have today with credit cards," says TD's Visa chief David Livingston. "It will take five years to do it in debit cards."

Consolidation

CIBC's Vessey, who is in charge of the seventh-largest Visa operation in the world, anticipates a consolidation of the credit card market in Canada. In the high-cost card business, big is beautiful, he says, anticipating that fringe players, like the gas card issuers, will leave the business. They don't make any money and consumers want to put all their spending on one or two cards. Vessey predicts that the field will be reduced to 10 or so players:

the big banks, the three biggest retailers and a couple of others.

How Competitive Are Credit Cards?

There is a huge debate over this question. The more competitive they are, of course, the better for consumers. On the face of it, most of the cards are not competitive at all, since historically they have posted similar rates, all of them – until recently – extremely high. Critics point to an oligopoly of the big banks and suggest collusion. There is little question that when interest rates go up, credit card rates follow quickly – much more quickly than they move down when interest rates head down.

Financial institutions respond that, while the credit on cards is the most expensive form of credit for consumers, it is by far the most expensive for them to provide. Administrative costs are high, because they have to process millions of transactions, many for amounts as small as a few dollars. Unlike many other loans, card debt is unsecured by collateral, so write-offs are high, ranging from 1 to 2 per cent in good times to 3 to 4 per cent when times are bad. People in financial difficulty will first pay their mortgage, out of fear of losing their home, and then their car loan – given how important cars are in most people's lives – rather than their card balances. Issuers further justify their high rates by pointing out that they collect no interest during the grace period and none from those cardholders who pay their balances in full.

Let's say the bank charges 15 per cent interest on its balances. Five per cent covers the grace period and "free riders"; 2 per cent might cover write-offs, leaving 8 per cent for the cost of funds and profit. Fees would cover operating costs. Of course, the issuer also receives the discount or interchange from the merchant. Banks and other financial institutions argue that similar card rates, as with mortgage rates, reflect intense competition, rather than collusion. They say the card business is fiercely competitive because the barriers against switching cards are among the lowest of any consumer good or service.

There is no evidence of explicit collusion. Rather, there are many indications of increasing competition, in terms of both benefits and interest rates. That's not to say that high rates in the past have been justified; the very fact that some financial institutions are at long last offering discount cards suggests the opposite. The banks' complaints about high write-offs are similarly difficult to swallow, coming as they do from the very institutions that encourage consumers to run up big balances (by requiring only token minimum payments) and that launch mass mailings of unsolicited applications to consumers. (The old practice of sending out "live ammo" – unsolicited cards ready to be used – has long ended and is illegal in the United States.) For smart consumers, what counts is that the banks and other institutions really do want your business, which makes the usual "shop around" advice more than just a cliché.

High rates have attracted criticism on both sides of the border from consumer groups and politicians. The U.S. Senate voted in November 1991 for a cap on card rates of 14 per cent, which triggered a huge sell-off on the New York Stock Exchange. President George Bush threatened to veto the measure, which put an end to it. Only one of the three parliamentary committees in this country recommended a ceiling on rates. The most recent accepted the banks' argument (or threat) that a cap would force them to put fees up and tighten credit standards, thereby cutting off the less creditworthy, such as minorities and single mothers. The committees focused largely on recommending greater disclosure and a more uniform system of calculating charges. Consumers were left to fend for themselves.

There is a final, compelling argument in this debate that

should serve as a warning to anyone who carries a credit card. An American academic recently set out to discover why bank card rates remained consistently high in the 1980s, even though the cost of funds to the banks was falling.[4] With over 4,000 firms competing for card business and little government regulation, the market looked like an ideal battleground for real competition. But there was no significant competition on rates, and the banks made from three to five times as much on cards as on their other lines of business. Was there something "uniquely pathological" about credit cards that led to this failure of competition? Was there collusion? Though the study found no explicit collusion, its conclusion was almost as disturbing. Consumers, who often complained about card fees and would go to great lengths to get a slightly greater return on a GIC, were quite willing to pay high interest rates on the cards. While they did not intend to carry balances and even denied that they did, they nonetheless continued to do so and to pay the prevailing rates. It's this irrationality that smart consumers must avoid.

How to Use Your Credit Card
Like it or not, credit cards have become a late-twentieth-century form of currency. A few people have managed to avoid them, but most have succumbed to the convenience and lure of instant, free credit (even if the reality has yet to catch up with them). Used properly, cards can be useful; in some circumstances they have become virtually essential, as anyone renting a car or booking a hotel room over the phone has discovered. Acquiring a card in your own name and using it responsibly is also one way to establish a credit rating.

Types of Users
The first step in getting maximum benefit from cards at mini-

mum cost is to determine what kind of card user you really are. Don't kid yourself. Take a simple test. Get out the last 12 statements for each of your cards and see what you paid in transaction and annual fees and interest charges. Add a twelfth of the annual fee to your average monthly interest payments. Decide whether you are strictly a convenience user (or "free rider") who always pays off the full balance by the due date; a credit user most or all of the time; or a combination user, who pays in full most months but carries a balance a couple of times a year, typically after Christmas, a big holiday or a large purchase.

About 20 per cent of Canadians regularly pay in full each month, another 30 per cent carry balances from time to time, and somewhat more than 50 per cent seldom if ever pay the total owing. Some are hell-bent to run each card to its limit till the day they die, leaving their executors to write the final, full repayment cheque. The average balance outstanding is around $800 for regular cards and $1,200 for premium cards. If you have the discipline to move from being a credit user to a convenience user, great. Most people don't, regardless of what they say. Of course, some are forced to find religion because they have creditors phoning in the middle of the night. The majority of cardholders, however, stick with the payment habits they've developed and can most easily improve their positions by ensuring they have the most suitable card.

Convenience users

In a perfect world, we'd all pay in full every month, waiting till the due date to take full advantage of the grace period. Free riders take the *bank* to the cleaners instead of getting taken, smug in the realization that their unwillingness to pay any interest puts rates up for those less organized than themselves. The banks pretend they support this responsible use of cards, but of course they prefer cardholders who routinely pay the absolute minimum and remain on the hook for life. (With card interest at 15.75 per cent, it would take 66 months and $313 in interest to pay for a $1,000 purchase by paying the monthly minimum.)

There is usually a choice between low-fee/high-interest cards and high-fee/lower-interest cards. Since free riders don't care about interest rates, they want a card with a low fee, or no fee at all. Over the years, I have tried to remain in the convenience category; I have a Bank of Montreal standard-issue, no-fee, no-transaction-charge MasterCard, the card the bank built its franchise on. The fact that rates are high on the card (15.75 per cent, currently nine percentage points above prime) worries me not a jot, since I pay in full every month. Other cardholders are in effect paying for my 21 free days of credit from the statement date, the grace period on the card. (Of course we all pay indirectly, since the merchant who accepts the card has to increase prices to pay his fees.)

Credit users/combination users

"It [a credit card] is an expensive way to borrow money," Bank of Montreal vice-chairman Alan McNally told the parliamentary committee, and who could disagree?[5] But don't let your self-esteem fall too far if you regularly carry a balance. People in your category tend to be more, not less, affluent and educated, and are in that much sought-after 33- to 45-year-old bracket. They too want convenience, albeit at a great cost. "Contrary to the fiction that goes around, it is not Joe Q. Lunch Pail Public who tends to run up debts on his Visa or MasterCard," Roy Fithern, the Royal Bank's senior vice-president for card services, said in 1991. "If you looked at their lifestyles and their income you would say, why don't they order this a little better?" [6]

Why indeed? In fact, what you really pay is even more than

the posted rate, and it's critical to those who use their cards to borrow money (as well as to the banks, who get from 30 to 60 per cent of their revenues from interest charges, depending on how much they get in fees). First, annual and transaction fees are part of your real cost, with an $18-a-year fee adding $1.50 a month. Second, partial payments on bank cards are only partially good. Say your balance is $1,000 and you pay $900. You will be charged interest on the entire amount from the date the purchases were posted to your account until the final $100 is paid off. In other words, you're paying interest on the $900 you paid as well as on the $100 you didn't. Your grace period disappears.

For those who carry balances, a retail card with a posted rate of 28.8 per cent can actually be cheaper than a bank card. Retail cards (except in Quebec and for Canadian Tire) subtract payments of 50 per cent or more from your balance before interest is determined. Does the way the banks calculate interest sound insidious? It is. In the words of Don Blenkarn, former Conservative MP and chairman of the finance committee that studied credit cards, it's a "dishonest" and "embarrassing" example of double-dipping.[7]

Solutions

Once you realize how much plastic is really costing you, the obvious solution is to avoid ever carrying a balance. Or to reduce the purchases you make on credit cards. But let's be more realistic.

It may even be that you don't care what you are paying for your credit cards; you know you're paying for convenience, and you are happy to do so. "I don't think this [getting a credit card] is necessarily a rational decision people make," says David Livingston, senior vice-president, Visa, for TD Bank. "It's not a financial decision they make. Convenience and simplicity become factors." He says the average person sees interest charges as the cost of convenience. "It comes down to: what's your time worth? If the credit card costs you $150 a year ... what do you want to go through to save $150 a year?"

If this is all you pay, and you are happy with it, congratulations. But if you want to reduce the amount you fork over, however much it is, here are some tips.

• If you carry a balance, pay what you can as soon as possible to reduce your average daily balance, which is the figure used to calculate the following month's interest charges.

• If you continually run up big balances, sit down with the loans manager at your branch and establish a more efficient way to manage your debts. Take the banks at their word when they talk about the importance of "relationship banking," their attempt, after years of neglect, to establish personal relationships with regular customers. You want a lending arrangement that allows you to borrow at rates well below credit card rates. Consider an instalment loan to pay off large, outstanding balances. More desirable is a personal line of credit, so you don't have to keep going back to your branch every time you need to borrow. Canada Trust has a PowerLine MasterCard with a line of credit at rates as low as prime. If you have overdraft protection, check to see if an overdraft is cheaper than paying interest on the balance on your card.

• If you've been spending a lot on your card but have always paid back at least the monthly minimum, your bank might, without being asked, increase your credit limit. If you're worried about your debts and lack discipline, contact the bank to refuse the credit increase. Many people spend to their limit, whatever it is.

• It's a foolish idea to dip into savings and investment funds to pay bills. But if you really are living in credit card hell, check to see if you have any savings or investments that yield much less than the rate on your card debt.

• Don't get cash advances on your card. Even the banks don't encourage the practice. The rates are as high as other card rates and there is no grace period. You start paying interest the moment the money is in your hand.

• If it's clear that you are regularly going to carry a balance and your credit record or income is not good enough to merit a PLC, apply for a discount card, which carries a lower interest rate than regular cards. Though the annual fee will be higher and the grace period may have disappeared, you will save money in the long run if your balances are big enough. Most discount card brochures will give you an idea of whether a discount card will save money for someone with your spending and payment habits. You should qualify if you've had a regular card for at least a year and have a good repayment record. Discount cards come with cheques to pay off other debts, including balances on other, higher interest credit cards. Remember that you don't need to have any relationship with a particular bank to apply for its card.

(The introduction of discount cards led to a wonderful *crise de conscience* among financial institutions that was emblematic of the difference between the 1980s and the 1990s. Do cardholders want their friends to know they have a discount card? "Customers told us they don't want a card that says: I don't pay off my bills every month," said a National Trust executive. In contrast, a Bank of Nova Scotia official said their card "shows that customers appreciate good value."[8] As a result, National Trust doesn't offer a differently designed card, while Scotiabank does.)

• Try leaving your credit cards at home. Use cash. You will quickly recall how cathartic it is to peel off a roll of twenties to pay for a purchase. Using cash makes you stop spending once the money is gone; it also reduces your impulse spending, for example, when you discover you're not carrying enough cash on the day you spot that unneeded Donna Karan dress or Italian leather attaché case. Paying cash also ends the fear and loathing that can rear its head just before the arrival of your card statement, which you know will list all those moments of weakness you had almost succeeded in forgetting. Ask merchants if they offer a discount for cash. Many do. They prefer cash because it means they don't have to pay a fee to the card people on your purchase.

• Always pay at least your minimum balance. If you don't, you could lose your access to an ABM and whatever frequent flyer points you had accumulated that month.

What Cards Should You Carry?

Many credit card holders have more cards than they need. It costs them a lot more money than they think it does. That's why it's so important to add up what your cards actually cost you each year.

Consumers often acquire cards with little forethought. ("Out of the blue an application arrived in the mail and I thought, why not?") In the last couple of years, many have smartened up and cut back their debt levels and number of cards. J. Douglas Goold, American Express gold card member since 1982, decided after more than a decade of occasional use and rising fees to cut his card in half. I also got rid of my card as a quiet protest to American Express's ham-fisted response to some small restaurants who rebelled against Amex's merchant fees, which can run as high as 3.5 per cent. Have I been able to leave home without it? You bet. With $130 more in my pocket than when I was paying the annual fee. I survive just fine without the baubles Amex sells through the mail, from grandfather clocks to "Front of the Line" theatre tickets, and I have yet to encounter a business that won't deal with me because I lack an American Express card. And despite my clearly diminished status, now that I've left the Amex "club," my friends still speak to me. Amazing.

The right number and type of cards for you will depend on your circumstances. The starting point for most people is the standard Visa ("It's the only card you need," say the ads) or MasterCard ("Your card for life"). Check to see if the bank or trust company you use offers any breaks to its own customers. Canada Trust and Royal Trust, the latter now part of the Royal Bank, have preferential packages for those who use a variety of their services. Business people, particularly those who entertain and travel, will probably want a separate corporate or entertainment and travel card. The card fee can be written off as a business expense.

If you want to save money on fees and if you have the discipline, restrict your household to one card. Good luck on this one.

Premium cards

Whatever prestige might have been attached to these cards is now gone, another victim of the excesses of the 1980s. In the 1990s, in the words of *The Wall Street Journal*, we're living in the "meat loaf decade." So much for paying $165 a year for TD's Gold Elite card, even though it offers a 1 per cent "dividend reward" on card purchases. It sells itself as "an achievement ... a card that recognizes your stature." You don't care about your stature in the land of plastic, you care about saving money for the things you really want or need.

What value, if any, is left in cards characterized by high fees? Obviously, many consumers perceive value – or benefits – there, since the number of gold card holders has soared in recent years.

Premium cards, most of which are gold cards (such as Visa's Aerogold card), offer higher credit limits than ordinary cards. But I see on my MasterCard statement that I have a credit limit of $6,300, which was recently and mysteriously increased from $5,000. To the best of my recollection I have never had a credit card balance anywhere near $6,300, or even $5,000, and I certainly didn't ask for an increase. The point is that you don't need to pay extra fees for a snazzy card just to increase your credit limit. If that is what you want, a history of increased spending, a reasonable credit record and a letter to the card issuer will probably secure it for you. So why pay more?

Premium cards come with bells and whistles. As a general principle, it is a bad idea to get a card simply for the added benefits, unless there is one in particular – such as a good frequent flyer plan, if you fly a lot – that really makes sense for you. Don't be one of the many who pay for the benefits and leave them unclaimed; or who spend more to accumulate more points; or who pay far more in fees and interest charges than they ever gain in benefits. And as many Snowbirds, who escape for part of the year to Florida or Arizona, have discovered, you might have a benefit (such as out-of-country health insurance coverage) one day and have it severely restricted or even withdrawn the next.

If you have a good credit rating, are a sizable spender and are attracted to a premium card, talk to the issuer of your existing card about an upgrade – and don't hesitate to ask for a discount on the fee, particularly if you have your mortgage or RRSPs with that institution. Holders of some gold cards, such as Bank of Montreal's gold MasterCard, qualify for a discount on personal loans.

Affinity cards

The banks and other financial institutions imported this marketing idea from the United States in the late 1980s, to increase their card memberships, particularly among the well-to-do. They have not done well here, since Canadians appear to have weaker ties than Americans to particular institutions. The cards give holders the opportunity to identify themselves with and support a group, institution or charity, whether it's Ducks Unlimited, McGill University alumni or Care Canada. (The Elvis card, which sports a likeness of the king, is not available in Canada.)

Unless these cards make you feel good, they make little sense. Fees tend to be higher. In my view, they represent an unholy and often tasteless alliance of Mammon and good works, with Mammon predominating. ("This card saves lives," Canada Trust claims shamelessly in its UNICEF Canada affinity card ad.) The sponsoring groups receive modest benefits, usually around 0.25 per cent of the purchase amount, though card issuers are remarkably taciturn on the subject. They are eager to say they care, but not so eager to say how much. Hence a $100 purchase means a quarter in the till of your group. If you really care about a cause, particularly one that's a registered charity, you could skip the card and write them a cheque for considerably more than the annual fee and come out even, since your contribution to a registered charity is tax deductible.

Auto cards

Introduced in the spring of 1992, auto cards allow the holder to earn a rebate, which currently starts at 5 per cent on all card transactions, towards the purchase or lease of a new vehicle from a particular manufacturer. Issuers wanted to strengthen the loyalty of traditional buyers and get others, who wouldn't normally have considered their products, to at least have a look. The cards have proven to be wildly popular. TD's GM Visa card attracted more than half a million applicants in the first few months. The bank was so overwhelmed by the response that it managed to send applications to children and to issue a card to a cat named Mookie.

In October 1993, I received an unsolicited "preapproved invitation" for a TD GM Visa card with a preapproved credit limit of $2,500, in the name of Douglas J. Gould (surname misspelled and initial misplaced). In the spring of 1994, I received an application form for the same card, with no preapproval, in the name of John Goold (wrong given name, right surname). Meanwhile, CIBC was enticing evil triplet John D. Goold with a Ford Gold Visa card. I will obviously stick with Douglas J. Gould, the brother with the highest credit standing.

I mentioned the errors to TD's David Livingston, whose signature was on the letters accompanying the TD GM Visa offers. "Well, we bought lists, and that's the problem when you buy lists," he replied.

TD limits the rebate to $500 a year to a maximum of $3,500 over seven years, while CIBC lets you build up a rebate of $700 a year to $3,500 over five years (their gold card ups the ante to $1,400 a year to a limit of $7,000 over five years). Which card is best for you will depend on how much you are likely to spend, and hence how quickly you can earn the rebate, and how soon you plan to buy a new car. Both banks allow cardholders to transfer their rebates to supplementary cardholders or to family members living under the same roof.

Interest rates are the same as for the non-auto versions of the cards. The lack of fees is the key to the success of TD's card. Many consumers far prefer a low fee to a low interest rate on a card, because they can control the amount they pay out in interest but can do nothing to lessen the fee. Issuers love auto cards because holders spend more on them – the American experience indicates as much as double – and use them to consolidate their spending in order to build up their rebate.

It seems unlikely that auto cards will be a big help to many people, though the two issuers say they have no idea how many people will buy cars using the rebates. If you have an ordinary bank card and the thought of accumulating credits towards an auto appeals to you, there's no reason not to exchange cards. Consider, however, that the rebate plans lock you into buying from a particular manufacturer, whose offerings may have changed by the time you are ready to buy. That's not a problem if you religiously buy from the same manufacturer every time you go car shopping, or are at least willing to consider the offerings of the car company whose card you carry.

Note very carefully that you will need to spend a small fortune with an auto card to make it worthwhile. The average annual charges on a card are around $3,200; a cardholder intent on taking advantage of the full $3,500 rebate would need to ring up a whopping $70,000 in purchases. You will either have to wait 20 years for your dream car or start charging round-the-world trips on your card. There is no time limit on the rebate offer, but if you're an average spender, either you or the automobile may be obsolete by the time you are ready to choose your new vehicle.

Here is the key point if you decide to take advantage of your rebate. Don't tell the dealer in advance that you have the points; it could lessen your negotiating clout, even though the rebate is paid for by the car company, not by the dealer.

Meanwhile, the Bank of Montreal is offering MasterCard holders who have a deposit account with the bank the chance to work towards a $2,500 rebate on the purchase of their first house, as long as they arrange their mortgage with the bank. Once again, you would have to spend $50,000 over five years to get the maximum benefit (or less if you have a partner with a separate card to help you out). While it's a perk for the bank's MasterCard holders, it hardly justifies switching cards. Why tie yourself into a particular mortgage lender when the competition among lenders is so intense?

Benefits and Features

Think twice before getting a card simply to take advantage of the bells and whistles. The real value of a credit card is to provide convenience and to extend credit, not to provide warranties on merchandise, or collision insurance. And not only can benefits be extended one day and withdrawn the next, but you may not even have the benefits you think you do. Some premium cardholders have been upset, for example, to discover that free collision insurance on rental cars – another area, incidentally, where benefits have been cut back – does not extend beyond North America. All this underlines the necessity of carefully reading your cardholder's agreement – assuming the "mouse" type isn't too tiny to read (one executive I interviewed laughingly referred to his bank's larger "rat" type) – since it may contain nasty surprises in the form of charges or exclusions.

A story from the fall of 1993 graphically illustrates the need to read and understand all benefit agreements. Rollie and Julie Secord of Timmins, Ontario, became locked in a fight with the Canadian Snowbird Association over a $95,000 (U.S.) bill for a quintuple heart bypass Mr. Secord had in Florida. The couple, who had paid more than $1,000 for the association's insurance, admitted they had not read the policy. At issue was an exclusion for health conditions that developed within 90 days of applying for coverage.

Read your cardholders' agreement and throw it into your holiday bag, because it's on vacation that you are most likely to need the benefits your cards offer. Know the details of any other insurance coverage you have, since it might take precedence over card coverage. Your house insurance may cover some losses that you suffer while on holiday, for example, while your employer or union may provide coverage you are not aware of. Find out. You could discover that getting a premium card for the sake of insurance or other benefits is unnecessary, since you are already adequately covered. (Another example: warranty coverage may offer nothing beyond the warranty extended by the seller of a product.)

Travel insurance

Since the fall of 1991, government health plans such as Ontario's (OHIP) have drastically cut payouts for health costs incurred outside the country. At the same time, Blue Cross and other insurers have increased their rates, in some cases doubling or tripling them, in response to skyrocketing health care costs in the United States and a weakening of the Canadian dollar. Premium cards have sharply reduced or even ended their benefits, and increased age and other restrictions. Provincial health ministries say it's essential to get additional coverage for trips outside Canada, even for an afternoon's shopping. Here are some points to consider:

• Are you insured under your card only if you use it to pay for your travel?

• When you compare travel insurance packages, whether offered with cards or on their own, consider both price and benefits. You generally get what you pay for. Choose a plan that has benefits that suit whatever medical needs you can anticipate – something you might discuss with your doctor. Are problems that arise from existing medical problems covered?

• Do you get to choose your own hospital?

• Is transportation back to Canada provided, if necessary?

• Do you have to pay the hospital or doctor directly and get compensation later? Bills of $20,000 to $30,000 are not uncommon.

• The plans are complicated. Don't hesitate to ask questions and get answers in writing.

• How long are you covered? Can you extend or renew your coverage if you decide to prolong your stay outside the country?

• Be sure your plan has a toll-free emergency number.

• Contact your plan as quickly as you can once it is clear you will incur medical expenses. Keep all your receipts and documents to validate your claim.

• The Canadian Life and Health Insurance Association produces a helpful pamphlet entitled Health Insurance for Travellers. Contact 1 Queen St. E., Suite 1700, Toronto, Ont. M5C 2X9, 1-800-268-8099, or 777-2344 from the Toronto area.

Other contacts include: the Canadian Association of Retired Persons at (416)363-2277, and the Canadian Snowbird Association at 391-9000 in the Toronto area or 1-800-265-3200 outside it.

Other travel hints

Hotel and car rental agencies sometimes demand large deposits on your credit card, and that can reduce the amount of credit you have available. For example, the $1,000 the rental car people ask for will reduce to $4,000 your $5,000 limit. Try to settle on an amount in line with the likely cost. Have them keep the transaction slip in a drawer until your return, when it should be ripped up. If you encounter a serious problem, phone the Visa or MasterCard customer service line.

Credit cards are a good way to pay for merchandise in a foreign country. Visa or MasterCard might be able to intervene and help you with a vacation problem, such as a dishonest retailer who sold you goods on your card. And you can more easily document your spending by using a card. Cards tend to offer reasonably fair currency conversion rates, though the rate you will get is not the one applying at the time of purchase, but the one in effect when the transaction is posted to your account. You should pay less than the 1 per cent that is charged for most travellers' cheques, and escape the large commission that is taken in some countries when you use those cheques abroad. Another advantage over travellers' cheques: no worry about buying too much foreign currency and having to convert it back into Canadian dollars, thus paying another set of charges.

Bank cards are another increasingly popular option, given the proliferation of ABMs abroad, which can spit out the local currency at a reasonable rate of exchange. Don't overuse the ABMs, however, since there will be a $2 or so fee per transaction.

Frequent flyer programs/air miles

The two major Canadian airlines introduced frequent flyer programs into Canada from the United States in 1984, in an attempt to lock in customers and increase travel by air. They have proven popular, if expensive for airlines. Air Canada offers Aeroplan and Canadian Airlines International runs Canadian Plus, in alliance with other airlines around the world. The programs have become breathtakingly complicated, with consumers able to exchange miles flown for free air travel and gifts. Car rental outfits, hotels and retailers have got into the act, making it almost a full-time job just keeping track of what's available.

Card firms began to team up with airlines in 1987 to create cards that awarded frequent flyer points, to attract spending that might have gone on competitors' cards. They seem to have succeeded. Most card programs, such as CIBC's Aerogold Visa, which is linked to Air Canada, are frequent shopper cards. They award a point for each dollar charged on plastic, with the points redeemable for free flights, prizes, or – in the case of American Express – "great experiences," the ultimate in these apparently being "Power breakfast with [unnamed celebrity]." (They have the power and you get the breakfast.) Some guidelines:
• Before you plunk down the high annual fee for a premium frequent flyer card, estimate how much you are likely to fly in the next year. Consider the card fee part of the cost of your "free" trips, particularly if you acquired the card specifically to rack up points.
• If you fly a lot and are keen to build up your points, consider getting a card that has agreements with other companies (a

rental car company, a hotel chain, etc.) that you are happy to do business with. Then use those companies as much as you can.

• That said, don't bend your itinerary out of shape or make purchases simply for the sake of points.

• A lot of points go unclaimed. Make sure you are aware of the points you have or are entitled to. Because the programs change so frequently, make sure – annoying as it is – to read carefully all the documents you are sent.

The Air Miles Reward Program – "Shop like always. Fly like never before" – is entirely separate, and miles earned through it are not interchangeable with frequent flyer points. Consumers can earn miles towards free flights or gifts by making purchases at participating sponsors, whether or not they use a credit card. The single bank participant is the Bank of Montreal, which awards one travel mile for each $20 charged to an Air Miles MasterCard (which has a $35 annual fee), alongside whatever miles the sponsor credits. The program, a "loyalty"-based marketing program aimed at keeping existing customers, was introduced in Canada in 1992, after its introduction in the United States and Britain by Boston-based Loyalty Management Group Inc.

The good news is that the program is free. The bad news is that it's complicated because each participant decides how many miles it will award for the amount spent. Shell Canada, for example, coughs up a travel mile for a $20 purchase. Canada Safeway will give you 250 travel miles a year if you buy $80 in groceries a week at their stores. At that rate, you will have to shop at Safeway for more than two years to earn a Toronto – Montreal return ticket.

The Air Miles program continues in Canada and Britain, but it collapsed in the United States in May 1993, because there were too few corporate sponsors, and cardholders complained that the miles were too hard to use. "You had to buy 30,000 pounds of dog food for an upgrade," quipped Robert McKinley, president of RAM Research Corp., a card research firm based in Frederick, Maryland.[9] The same problem of building up miles is true in Canada. If you have accumulated a lot and are pondering whether to redeem what you have, consider the program's demise south of the border. What might happen to your miles if the same happens here? Poof! Use them now, just in case.

Card safety

Safeguard your credit cards. "Credit card crime has become the crime of the decade," *Canadian Banker* warned in 1992. Canada is one of the worst countries in the world for credit card fraud. Losses for 1993 were $55 million, and 55,000 Canadians were the victims of card fraud. Groups like the Big Circle Boys, part of a criminal organization from the Far East (which is based in Toronto but whose efforts extend even to Newfoundland), are alleged to have been busy minting fake cards and using the proceeds to finance illegal gambling and drug activities. In the spring of 1994, police smashed two of its gangs, whose members are accused of being responsible for a staggering one-fifth of the world's phony credit cards.

Organized crime is behind most credit card fraud, which comes in two flavours. Either completely counterfeit cards are made through a silk-screen process and then encoded with actual customer data, or real cards are reimpressed with a new set of numbers. In May 1992, police in Winnipeg arrested three individuals for using 10 counterfeit cards. Eight of the cards were real, with the magnetic strip on the back electronically changed to include the data of another genuine card, while the other two were totally counterfeit. The enterprising, "shop till you drop" holders of the cards had used them to buy more than $50,000 worth of goods in three days in Winnipeg, after spending what the police termed an "excessive amount" with the same cards in Vancouver.[10]

You never know when and where your cards will go missing. I once had my wallet and cards stolen from the basement of a Catholic church in Edmonton, where I was covering a sit-in by refugees from El Salvador, after I carelessly left them in my unattended coat. (The culprit, who was never caught, walked into a bedding store in a strip mall and asked the owner if she would cash a large cheque, using my ID. She said she would only do so if he bought something. So he did. A mattress. He got some cash, and I was awakened the following Saturday morning by two men carrying a mattress up my walk.)

Unless there is clear negligence on your part (I would qualify), your liability is usually limited to $50 on a lost or stolen card, as long as you immediately report its disappearance. Most disappeared cards have not disappeared at all, but have fallen into the hands of a family member, slipped down the back of the sofa, or been eaten by the dog. We all pay for negligence and theft, indirectly at least, since it increases costs and hence prices.

Because of security concerns, the number on your card contains little information beyond the type of card and the part of the country the holder lives in. The latter is included simply for customer service purposes.

Here are some tips for safeguarding your credit cards:
• A thief doesn't need your signature. As you will know if you've ever paid by card over the phone, a card number and expiry date will suffice. One might well ask what "signature on file" means when you get a copy of your receipt, because in most cases they have no such thing. Keep your number secret and destroy all carbons. Don't give your number to anyone over the phone unless you're sure the listener can be trusted. Since some credit cards can be used with a personal identification number to draw money from an ABM, keep your card and your PIN separate. And keep your PIN secret from everyone, including your bank, which will

not phone and ask you for the number. (Nor will a "bank inspector" or police officer phone you and ask you to withdraw money, as part of a scheme to catch a crooked bank employee. "Beware of the phony bank inspector," warns the Canadian Bankers Association.)

• You are legally responsible for your cards, so don't lend them out. And don't leave them in a hotel room, or lying around or in an unlocked drawer at work, the most popular location for card theft. Glove compartments are also a bad choice; while I was writing this chapter, thieves ransacked every car in the neighbourhood in the middle of the night, finding precisely nothing in my (carelessly unlocked) vehicle, but making off with a credit card found in a neighbour's glove box.

• Use your driver's licence rather than a credit card for identification. If you do show your card, don't let anyone copy down the number. Merchants aren't allowed to take your number for identification purposes, under the terms of their agreements with Visa and MasterCard. They also can't put your bill on a card if the cheque that you give them bounces.

• Save your receipts. Check them against your statement as soon as you receive it. Report any discrepancies immediately.

• Take advantage of any free card registration services. Otherwise, keep your own registry of card names and numbers, and emergency phone numbers, in a safe place.

• If you have a lot of cards, don't carry them all as a matter of course. If, for example, you have a Holt Renfrew card that you use only for Christmas presents, leave it locked away at home except in December.

In short, treat your credit cards like cash.

ABM safety

Safety at bank machines is a large and growing concern in

Canada, as it has long been in the United States. Cities like Toronto and Vancouver are trying to adjust to what many citizens perceive as rising levels of crime and violence. Here are some ABM tips:

• Don't write down your PIN; memorize it.

• If you don't like the location, lighting or look of a machine, go to another one.

• Try to shield your PIN when you conduct your transaction.

• Take your transaction slip with you, and hang on to it for your records and in case there's a dispute.

• Don't dawdle at the machine, smacking your lips as you count your twenties.

• Call your bank immediately if your card is lost or stolen.

This advice may remind you of your parents' hands-on-hips homilies. But following it will, at the very least, spare you the rigmarole required to replace lost or stolen cards.

Summary

• Determine what kind of card user you are by adding up what you have paid for cards over the last 12 months.

• Minimize or eliminate the balances you carry. At the very least, always pay the minimum.

• If you do carry balances, lessen the interest you are paying by getting a personal line of credit or a discount card.

• Be a devil. Leave your cards at home and try cash.

• Before getting a premium card, ask yourself if the higher fee is justified by the benefits you will gain.

• Read the fine print in your cardholder's agreement.

• Safeguard your cards.

Mr. Varone, if you had to start
all over again, if you had to begin
a new career and to negotiate again
with bankers, what would you wish for?

MP Yves Rocheleau

If I had to begin again,
I would become a bank.

Toni Varone, president,
the Varone Group, March 1994

CHAPTER 4

HOW TO GET A SMALL BUSINESS LOAN

Is the Bank Really Your Small Business Partner?

"Right now, in my view, banks are strip-mining the community," Susan Bellan, the proprietor of Toronto's Frida Craft Stores, told the House of Commons Industry Committee in early 1994. "They're like gigantic vacuum cleaners that vacuum out the savings of the community. Then when people in the community say they need this money back to keep their community strong, to create business, they say, oh no, too risky, too risky. Then they lend giant sums to foreign firms like Rogers Cable, which is equally risky but they get huge commissions."

Bellan may have been wrong about the ownership of Toronto-based Rogers, but she accurately reflected the sentiments of thousands of small business people across Canada. Like them, she has had unhappy experiences with banks, including a threat from the TD Bank in 1991 to call her paid-up loan. Unlike them, she did something about it, beginning with a phone call to the *Toronto Star*, which turned her saga into a front-page story.

"I have been consistently lectured that the TD does not like to lend to retail and is doing me a big favour," she wrote bank president Robin Korthals. "It seems to me, however, that I make a lot of money for the bank." In what seemed to be a confirmation of her point, Korthals replied that "in terms of the retail sector, normally, retailing does not require much bank credit"; after that he apologized for the high turnover of account managers she had been forced to deal with.

Thanks to the publicity, the TD backed off, and Bellan was soon in charge of banking issues for the Edmonton-based Canadian Organization of Small Business and an aggressive critic of the banks.

"It's disheartening to see two solitudes developing in Canadian society," Toni Varone, president of the Varone Group, a family business in the real estate and hospitality sectors, told the parliamentary committee, echoing a familiar refrain. "Record bank profits in the face of record unemployment and a devastation of small business."

Not that politicians have been any more sympathetic to the banks. Dennis Mills is Liberal MP for the Toronto riding of Broadview-Greenwood, which contains hundreds of small businesses. In a House of Commons debate, he said, "There are a lot of people in the financial sector of this country who approach their job in an intimidating, condescending fashion which puts the fear of God into a lot of their customers."

These sentiments are echoed by the Canadian Federation of Independent Business, a lobby group that represents 85,000 businesses across the country. "The banks basically never learned Marketing 101," says senior vice-president Brien Gray. "The first principle of marketing is that you try to understand what the customer's needs are. But the banks' position is: 'Here we are. We've got a dominant position in the market. We've got these products to sell. We assume they fit your needs. And by the way, it's a privilege for you to come in and ask us for some help.' With most service companies, it's the other way around."

Finally, consider these words from John Rodriguez, the fiery former NDP member for the northern Ontario riding of Nickel Belt, which includes Sudbury. The banks "suck out the money, send it someplace else, and when the community goes down, they're the first ones on the Greyhound out of town. I've seen that in Elliott Lake and I've seen it in other communities across the north. Why don't banks recognize that they are an integral part of the community and they do have a responsibility to the community?"

The anger of small business, the sector's comforting, motherhood appeal and the political clout of a million small businesses across the country explain why the sector's concerns became an issue in the 1993 federal election, and why the Liberals devoted ten pages of their Red Book platform to the sector. Early in 1994, they had the House of Commons Industry Committee review the problems small and medium-sized businesses have in gaining access to financing.

The banks quickly realized they had neither the support of government nor of public opinion (apart from an unfashionable editorial in *The Globe and Mail* entitled "The Banks That Can Say No"). Finance Minister Paul Martin warned that if legislation were required to ensure that small business had access to capital, there would indeed be legislation. Fearing increased regulation, the banks made a fast retreat, just as they had in the 1988 furore over high bank service charges (which will be discussed in Chapter 6).

A bad situation for the banks became worse after Michael Mackenzie, the federal bank regulator at the time, revealed to MPs in an *in camera* meeting in April 1994 (the results of which were made public) that bank lending to small business was decreasing, not increasing as the banks claimed. Total loans under $200,000 had fallen by mid-1993 to an annual $17.9 billion, from $21.7 billion in 1989. As a result, the usual bank bluster was interspersed with concessions, initiatives, promises to improve, and even admissions of guilt.

"We're acutely aware that these points of tension exist," CBA president Helen Sinclair told the committee. Even bank surveys "indicate that 30 per cent of our [small business] customers are dissatisfied with their banking relationship ... Mathematically, it may be a minority, but in business terms that's an important number. It's a number that I think the industry is determined to get down."[1]

Sinclair knew that the banks' own bible – the 371-page, 1990 Wynant-Hatch study published by the Western Business School in London, Ontario, funded by the CBA – found that 32 per cent of respondents were dissatisfied with their banks. And she knew that in a 1988 Canadian Federation of Independent Business (CFIB) survey, 3,600 small business people indicated that the banks "under-delivered" in nine areas (such as knowledge of the business person); and "over-delivered" in only two (convenient location and a wide range of banking services), neither of which they considered very important.[2] In July 1994, the CFIB released its biggest ever survey on banking issues, which polled 11,000 small and medium-sized businesses across Canada. It concluded that "financing conditions among the small- and medium-sized business community were as bad as ever, or worse."

So much for the banks' theme, "We're your small business partner," or for Scotiabank's widely used "Open for Small Business" ad, which shows a massive vault door slightly ajar, with a welcome mat in front of it.

"We could argue that we're not doing anything wrong – just protecting our depositors' money against unnecessary risk," Bank of Montreal president Tony Comper said in a refreshingly unbankerly speech on small business at Wilfrid Laurier University in Waterloo, Ontario, in 1993. "But for one thing, we wouldn't sound very convincing, given the industry's recent track record of multi-billion-dollar loan losses to corporate Canada. And for another thing, some of the [recent] criticisms were right on the mark." Comper even acknowledged that the banks regularly lagged behind trust companies and credit unions in the CFIB's customer satisfaction polls.

The Fundamental Problem

The banks' line is that the problem between themselves and small business is the result of poor communication. "Let's understand each other," implores the title of an article in a 1993 issue of *Canadian Banker*. The Western study concluded that small business doesn't understand the types of loans the banks are prepared to make, but blamed not just business, but also the banks, in part because of their misleading "partner" theme.[3]

The real problem, however, is more fundamental. The banks and small business have different values and cultures and, hence, agendas. The banks are ultra-conservative institutions that want to avoid risk. They are obsessed with preserving depositors' capital, which makes up 95 per cent of the money they lend out (the remainder is raised in the money markets). Entrepreneurs are by their nature risk takers. Because of the great risks involved in operating – let alone starting – a small business, they are optimists. They can't understand when others, particularly those – such as the banks – upon whom they rely, don't share their enthusiasm.

How conservative are Canadian banks? If you run a high-risk oil drilling company in Texas, you'll be able to find an American financial institution that will gladly lend you capital. The risk-adjusted price may be many percentage points above prime. In Canada, a similar company, particularly when the volatile energy sector is out of favour, will have a hard time finding a bank willing to extend financing. Rather than charge a company more than 3 or so points above prime, the risk-averse Canadian banks would prefer not to lend at all.

That's why the parliamentary committee was keen to discuss alternatives to bank financing, such as venture capital mutual funds. After all, Canada lacks not only higher-risk debt financing – loans from banks – but also equity financing, whereby institutions or wealthy individuals invest their capital in return for an ownership stake.

To be fair, the banks are in a lose-lose position. They are criticized when they lend to high-risk companies and end up taking huge write-offs; when they don't lend to them, they are criticized for failing to act in the public interest. Because of their enormous power and the privileges they get with their charters, they are expected to act in that interest. At the same time, they have a fiduciary responsibility to their shareholders and to their depositors. Few sympathize with a bank that pulls the plug on a business and puts people on the street, regardless of the circumstances.

"I am always being told by my bank that my loan is a privilege and not a right," summarizes critic Susan Bellan. "I think we have to make it clear to banks that their charters are a privilege and not a right." Compare that perspective to one expressed by Leo Legrove, former president of RoyNat, which was acquired by Scotiabank in 1994 and specializes in term loans to small business. "You have to realize that every individual in Canada does not have a God-given right to be in business and does not have a God-given right to get a loan from a bank. There are a lot of poor business people in Canada who should not be in business."[4]

Entrepreneurs on both sides of the border have complained about the "credit crunch" that started in 1990, when the most recent recession began. The Canadian banks reply that their small-business loan losses soared to an unacceptable 1.3 per cent of loan portfolios during the recession. In 1993 those losses were still running at 1.1 per cent, well above the 0.5 to 1.0 per cent considered acceptable. Given that target, loans officers say they have to be right 99 per cent of the time and hence can't take chances. They are well aware of the notoriously high failure rate for small businesses, particularly such types as Mom and Pop restaurants. Up to 15 per cent of small businesses disappear each year, and less than half survive a decade, thanks largely to poor management and insufficient equity.

Bankers know they will be punished for making bad loans; they may or may not be noticed for good ones. They are, however, increasingly paid to perform, with bonuses to account managers who open 15 new accounts worth $25 million in a year (to use one big bank as an example), and demands for explanations from those who fall far short of this target.

Despite the risks of small business lending, the banks' public commitment to it is not just an attempt to appease the politicians. Small business has been the fastest growing part of the economy and is an increasing source of fee income. Lending to it is one way the banks can try to capture the total banking needs of small business people, their families and even their employees.

And the small business sector's problems have been nothing compared with the wasteland that much of big business has become. CIBC announced in early 1994 that it was radically revising its corporate lending practices to lessen risk, after billions of dollars of losses over the years on companies like Dome Petroleum and the Reichmanns' Olympia & York.

As you would expect with large, rulebook-oriented organizations, the banks may have a corporate commitment to small business that hasn't quite filtered down to the troops in the field. Many on the front lines continue to view small business accounts as risky, time-consuming and marginally profitable.

The Importance of Small Business
There are two areas where the banks and small business do

agree. The first has become almost a mantra for bankers, economists, politicians, minority rights advocates, believers in Small Is Beautiful, the hopelessly sentimental – in a word, just about everyone. Small business is a vital, perhaps the most vital, part of the economy, and the biggest creator of jobs. It is also the area in which women have made the most progress.

This vitality is a function of the structural and demographic changes that are transforming Canada more fundamentally than at any time since the Second World War. Big businesses across North America, having grown fat and uncompetitive in an increasingly global market, stumbled in the early 1990s to a degree that would have been thought impossible only a few years ago. As a result of permanent layoffs (euphemistically called downsizings), more and more people have decided (or been forced) to set up their own businesses. Increasingly, both young people who have been frustrated by the traditional job market, and aging baby boomers who have been "rationalized" in mid-career, have struck out on their own, often starting businesses from their homes. This process has been made simpler by advances in technology, such as the new availability of fax machines, computers and modems. Many of these burgeoning businesses require little start-up capital. Half of all small business loans are for less than $50,000. Half the women who start businesses begin with less than $10,000.

Everyone agrees that the banks are critical to small business. In Canada, almost 85 per cent of small businesses rely upon the banks; this is one of the highest rates among industrialized countries. The banks are particularly important in smaller centres and in rural areas, where the alternatives are limited or non-existent.

The Basics

How small is small? A small business employs fewer than 50 full-time employees and has gross annual sales of less than $5 million. In fact, a small business can be, and often is, one person. The fastest growth is coming from businesses with five or fewer employees, which make up about three-quarters of the small businesses in Canada.

Banks provide two types of loans to small businesses. Term loans are advanced to acquire fixed assets, such as equipment. They have a fixed term, which can correspond to the life of the asset, and either a fixed or a floating interest rate. The loan is in part secured by the assets being acquired.

The second type of loan is a line of credit or an operating loan, used for operations and for emergencies. The interest rate is set at a premium to the prime rate. The terms can be changed from year to year. Operating loans are normally less expensive because they are repayable on demand and the interest rate floats, which allows the bank to increase the rate if its cost of funds rises.

The average rate one of the big banks was charging on operating loans in early 1994 was 2.2 percentage points over prime for loans to $25,000; 1.5 points for loans between $100,000 and $250,000 and 1.0 point for loans over $2 million. Term loans were 50 to 75 basis points above these levels. The CFIB's 1994 survey found that the average small business loan was 1.54 per cent over prime.

The banks lend according to the Five Cs of Credit, which we've discussed. They traditionally lend to business against collateral security and, to a lesser extent, cash flow, which indicates the ability to service debt. The emphasis is slowly changing in the direction of cash flow, for several reasons. First, the value of collateral can collapse in tough times, as happened with real estate in the late 1980s. Second, collateral is becoming less tangible and harder to value as technology grows in importance. A type of software that is worth millions one day may be outdated and worthless the next.

Shopping for a Bank

It's the banker, much more than the bank, that really matters. It's critical to choose a banker with whom you can establish a good long-term relationship. Ask around. Find out from business people in the area, from suppliers, from your accountant or lawyer, or from contacts in service clubs, who in the banking community might be able or willing to help you. Don't base your decision on something as trivial as the location of a branch.

Set up appointments with prospective bankers and don't be afraid to ask questions. Does the account manager have authority to lend the amount you need, or will the decision be made by someone else, someone to whom you won't be able to present your case? How long has the account manager been in the branch? And how long is he or she likely to stay? Try to get a sense of the banker's workload.

Is he or she knowledgeable about your type of business and interested in supporting it? A banker who has had bad experiences with clothing stores, for example, is likely to run for cover when approached with a proposal for a new one. The next banker approached is probably going to listen better. Sometimes all the branches in a region decide to limit their exposure in a particular sector.

Shop around. Unfortunately, most entrepreneurs don't. They think all banks and bankers are the same – they're not – and they fear that bankers will compare notes, particularly in small towns (this fear is valid, so do your shopping discreetly). While personal contact is always the most valuable method, check ads and brochures to find out what each institution is offering. The bumpf won't tell you the whole story, but it may give you some indication of who's keen to attract small business clients.

The Bank of Montreal, for example, has been keen, and by 1992 had risen sharply from last place on the CFIB's Report Card on Banking. The bank introduced a special small-business rate in 1991 and has launched a number of pilot projects, including one to finance high-tech or knowledge-based businesses that normally wouldn't qualify for loans. The Bank of Montreal has been rewarded with a larger market share.

Surprisingly, the CFIB's 1988 survey revealed that entrepreneurs get better results at ordinary branches than at commercial branches, which have been set up in recent years to deal exclusively with business clients. You and your business are more likely to be known at a regular branch. On the other hand, the staff at a commercial centre should be more knowledgeable about business and will have higher lending limits. The limit at a small, regular branch is typically $100,000 for new customers and $200,000 or more for established customers; the amounts can be increased by a certain percentage (20 per cent, in the case of one of the big banks) every year for existing customers without the application being forwarded to a higher authority.

Try a credit union, co-op or *caisse populaire*, particularly if you have a smaller business. It's no coincidence that the provinces with the best bank relationships are those, such as Quebec, where competition from smaller institutions is the strongest. Asked which institution had shown the biggest net improvement over the preceding three years on 15 characteristics, respondents to the CFIB's 1994 survey gave the highest ratings to the National Bank, credit unions/*caisses populaires*, and Bank of Montreal, in that order. Bank of Nova Scotia was mid-point on the list, while the Royal, CIBC, and TD were at the bottom, just ahead of trusts and finance companies. (The trusts – traditionally high on the list – were presumably victims of their almost complete disappearance at the hands of the banks.).

Continuity is important to small business people. If you do establish a good relationship with a loans officer, consider moving your business if he or she moves branches or even banks. A reasonable relationship with a banker counts for a lot. Don't give it up because of something minor like a disagreement over a fee or the offer of a slightly lower interest rate elsewhere. If, however, there is a serious problem, quietly go shopping. Almost half the business people who do, switch institutions.

If you live near the border and are unhappy with what Canadian banks offer, there's nothing to stop you from trying a bank on the U.S. side. Just make sure you know something about the American system – which is more fragmented, and more localized, and has more institutions that are willing to take risks – and that the bank you approach is well capitalized. Many banks aren't.

If you have clout, use it. The banks will compete for the accounts, particularly the larger ones, of more established, well-financed firms. Those firms can comparison-shop and negotiate the best terms. Your position is also stronger if you and your family have substantial deposits, RRSPs or mortgages at a branch, or would consider moving them there.

Remember, though, that many business people prefer to keep their business and personal banking at separate institutions, so the bank doesn't have a full view of their affairs and cannot dip into personal accounts (which they have a legal right to do) to offset business debts. Keeping the two separate will also leave you with a bargaining chip. The day you really need something from your banker, you may be able to get it by offering to move your personal banking to his or her branch.

How to Get a Loan
Start by getting as much equity as you can before you approach a

bank to negotiate debt. The more equity you have, the more you will impress a banker, the less debt you will require, and the better the terms. There are many sources of equity, including friends, relatives, partners, "angels" (private or "informal" investors with capital to invest), venture capitalists and governments.

Don't borrow too much. After all, you have to repay it. The ability to repay your loan in a timely fashion is the key to good relations with your bank. Bruce Druxerman, founder of the deli chain Druxy's, fought with CIBC for years, and while he often wished the bank had been more lenient, he admits that the constraints they put on his fast-growing business "made us a lot tougher."[5] A reasonable debt-to-equity ratio for a small business is 2:1 or 3:1.

Arrange your loan well before you need the money. If you know you will need more in six months' time, tell your banker. Banks don't like surprises. Borrow soon after you arrange the loan, even if you don't really need to, and repay promptly, to establish a good credit record. Pay down lines of credit when you have the chance, even if you know you will have to push them up again later.

The key to getting a loan is your business plan. "A business plan is the single most important document that you will produce in the lifetime of your company. It is the blueprint to your success," intones the Canadian Bankers Association's booklet *Financing a Small Business,* which is a good starting point for novice entrepreneurs. The shelves of larger bookstores groan under the weight of books on how to draw up a plan. The banks offer detailed brochures, and even disks, on the same topic; these have the advantages of being free and telling you exactly what a particular bank's expectations are. Here are a few general tips:

• Get help from your accountant or lawyer. Have your proposed business plan critically reviewed by someone who knows the business.

• Be optimistic, but not too optimistic. Bankers are conservative; they're like men who wear a belt and suspenders at the same time. Make realistic projections that will leave you room to outperform. Remember that the banks are not looking for fabulous growth. They simply want to know you will have the capacity to repay your debts.

• Include a section on risks. Your banker will admire your candour. In any event, he or she will be all too familiar with the risks and will want to talk about them. List your competitors and their strengths and weaknesses. Include a brief contingency plan, outlining your plans if the worst happens – as it often does.

• Include a green plan – that is, a discussion of any environmental problems your business will face and how you plan to deal with them. Increasingly, banks worry about environmental liability.

You may want to run your proposal by your banker before you proceed with a major business plan. "Sometimes customers come in and want to bounce a proposal off you, just to get a feel if they should spend the money, because it's not cheap to put a business plan together," says Tom Mesman, vice-president, credit, at the Bank of Nova Scotia. "We get inquiries in from branches, saying so-and-so was in and is thinking of putting an addition on the building they are buying and 'x' amount of equipment. The leverage is going to be a little high. Are we going to have an appetite for it? They'll go back to the customer and say, yes, we've got an appetite, or this is what you've got to do: you've got to get some appraisals, and put a business plan together."

The presentation of your plan is as important as the plan itself. Don't show up without an appointment or adequate preparation. Save the bold fashion statement for another occasion. Dress appropriately. You want to create a climate of confidence and to show that you have carefully thought through all aspects of your business. The banker will probably reach a decision in the first 10 minutes, so make it good. Think how often you've decided within a very few minutes whether you like someone and buy what they have to say.

The banker has every right to ask you tough questions, so be prepared for them. Do a test run with a friend before your session at the bank. What are the credit policies of your business? What impact would a 15 per cent increase or decrease in sales have? "Direct or pointed questions will need to be asked," Scotiabank's internal *Credit Presentation Handbook* says, "but in some areas a subtle approach should be taken with one point leading to another in the nature of the discussion." During a site visit, for example, "an innocuous question such as 'And where do you store your obsolescent inventory' almost forces a response detailing turn-over, supplies, etc."

Offer to follow up with any further information that is required, and do it quickly when asked. Invite the banker to visit your business, and to meet your key employees or partners. Keep your account manager up to date on your venture. Always provide information promptly. Delays are seen, often correctly, as a sign that the business is faltering.

The Issues

Many small business people believe that the banks have failed them. Many businesses have faced additional problems since 1990, the year the last recession began. The banks have been demanding more collateral at the very time that its value has been falling. Meanwhile, bank fees and government taxes, particularly payroll taxes, have increased.

The popular belief that the banks lend money only to those who don't need it is not without foundation. "When we needed money, when we started our business, the banks were difficult to deal with," one established company replied to the CFIB's 1988 survey. "Now that we don't need their help we are actively pursued."[6]

The banks have long been criticized for cutting back lending to particular sectors, such as retail, energy or real estate, at the very moment they most need financing. Restrictions can quietly be imposed in a variety of ways, such as by tightening the lending standards (by, for example, requiring more collateral) or by reducing the lending limit of branches. A branch might have a $200,000 loan limit, but a $50,000 limit for loans to restaurants, so that an application above that level has to be reviewed by a regional office. (Landscapers – "a couple of guys with a pickup truck and a few lawn mowers" – and restaurants are at the top of the list of high-risk borrowers.)

What riles small business the most about the banks? Surprisingly, the most visible feature of any loan, the interest rate, was cited in the CFIB surveys by only 5 to 10 per cent of small business people as their most significant concern. Borrowers seem happy with the speed with which their loans are processed and with their terms and conditions. Their main problems lie elsewhere. Topping the list, both in 1988 and 1994, were collateral requirements and fees and service charges. By 1994, credit availability had moved into the number-three spot, lending support to the CFIB's contention that a credit crunch was on.

Let's consider the top two concerns, and then turn to a number of other issues affecting the relationship between bankers and small business people.

Collateral

Collateral is widely considered both one of the biggest concerns of lenders and a problem for borrowers. "Usually they [the banks] ask for a guarantee of your shirt and everything else, including your car, your shorts and everything," one angry MP suggested in the Commons debate on small business loans in 1993. "Your kids," chipped in another.[7]

"I want to get $300,000," businessman Bob Goldstein complained at TD's 1994 annual meeting, at which bank executives were excoriated for their fat bonuses and their failure to support small business, "and I have to put my mother-in-law in the vault."

Small business loans are secured by collateral. The 1994 CFIB survey found that the average collateral security-to-loan ratio was 3.25:1, up substantially from the earlier survey.

The banks not unreasonably argue that they are looking at the liquidation value of security rather than its book value. If the business goes under, they want to be able to cover the loan by selling the security. The Western study analyzed problem loans and found that, despite holding collateral valued at almost double the loan amounts, the banks recovered only 64 per cent of the value of the loans when they liquidated the assets.

One lender I interviewed was in the throes of negotiations over the security provided by an Ottawa-area equipment dealer, whose business was winding down. The equipment had been appraised at $300,000, but the bank was offered only $100,000 for it. Revenue Canada suddenly appeared, claiming priority in the collection of sales tax, and another party "came out of the woodwork," saying it had a chattel (a mortgage on a movable possession) on some of the equipment. It looked like the bank would be lucky to walk away with $50,000.

Banks like tangible, saleable collateral, rather than difficult-to-value or hard-to-sell assets such as computers (which go obsolete quickly) or leasehold improvements. Banks such as the Bank of Montreal have acknowledged complaints that valuation procedures are becoming outdated in a knowledge-based society, and are starting to change their practices.

There is a related controversy over personal guarantees, which are required of most lenders, particularly for start-up businesses. The banks argue that by making a personal guarantee – by putting up assets such as your home, insurance and securities – you are showing commitment to your business and adding a big incentive to ensure it succeeds. The personal guarantee required is typically equal to, but can be greater than, the value of the loan, and is sometimes unlimited. "If someone is willing to personally guarantee a loan we're having a bit of a problem with, because it's a bit higher risk, that tells me a lot," says Scotiabank's Tom Mesman.

Bankers often demand less collateral for term loans, because the asset being purchased – machinery, equipment or a building – is used as part of the security. Expect the bank to apply these numbers when establishing collateral:

• 20 to 50 per cent of the stated value of inventory, depending on how saleable it is.

• 50 to 80 per cent of accounts receivable, depending on the type of product and the collection history.

• Up to 80 per cent of the assets purchased by a loan.

• 50 to 100 per cent of marketable securities.

• Up to 75 per cent of the fair market value of real estate (the crisis in that sector has, for the moment, made this benchmark unreliable).

Provide as little collateral as you can. If your position is strong, you should be able to hold some back. That way you will have more to offer if you need to borrow in the future. It will also serve as back-up if your business runs into trouble or if the value of your collateral drops. Once you develop a good relationship with your bank, and establish a record of making timely payments, ask to be released from personal guarantees. Once you've paid off a term loan, remember to ensure that you are formally released from all security obligations.

The bank's benchmarks are just guidelines. If you fall short on any of them, you may be able to bring something else into the equation to compensate.

Fees

Fees have always been a major grievance for small business people, and the problem is getting worse. A few years ago, the banks discovered fees were a relatively unmined source of revenue. As a result, they have enormously increased the number and size of the fees they charge. That has helped to buttress their bottom line.

Some banks trumpet that they have frozen or even reduced fees in recent years. But these are only "listed" fees, and a wide range of charges don't make the list.

There are three types of small business fees: loan application fees; activity fees, to cover specific transactions; and fees for loan management, such as monitoring. What is galling is that you appear to get nothing in return for the added costs. Taken together, fees can add a percentage point to the cost of a loan.

Fees also make comparison shopping more difficult. Because of their unpopularity and the negative press and political pressure they invite, the banks ensure they have a low visibility. When you don't know in advance the exact services for which you will be charged and the amount you will be asked to cough up, it's impossible to compare banks' total lending rates (defined as the interest rate charged plus fees).

Fees are often rather arbitrary and hence are negotiable. There can be big variations, even within the same bank. In the summer of 1993, Toronto-area branches of National Trust dropped a new $25-a-month "processing" fee in the face of complaints. This from a long-time small businessman whose complaints bore fruit: "I told him [a regional official for National Trust] I could switch to Canada Trust, where they will charge me a dollar and kiss me for the business. And I asked why I should refer clients to them for mortgages in the future." This from the backpedalling institution: "We admit it [the fee] was inappropriate, but it was not a corporate initiative. Some Metro-area branches initiated this ... People get overzealous when they are looking at ways to improve business."[8]

Find out in advance what fees you will face for your loan. Many banks offer packages, which could be cheaper. Keep track of all the fees you pay, so you can calculate the full cost of your loan. Doing your own accounts is a wonderful way to focus your attention on the true financial state of your business, and its costs.

Interest rates

The rates on small business loans fall within a fairly narrow range, with most customers paying a premium of less than 2 percentage points above prime. The banks track each other carefully on rates, though one account manager might give you a better rate than another, even at different branches of the same bank.

"There is no maximum," a Bank of Montreal executive told a Commons committee, regarding rates on lines of credit. "Obviously, beyond a reasonable rate, 2.5 per cent or so, one starts to question the validity of the deal."[9]

The rate is normally higher for newer, and hence riskier, businesses; for smaller loans, because the paperwork is similar to that for larger loans; and for rapid-growth companies, because of their apparent higher risk. If you are forced to pay a higher rate, don't expect to get a break on another aspect of the loan, such as collateral. If the banks perceive higher risk, they will demand more across the board.

High turnover of account managers

A surprising number of business people report that they have had three or more different account managers in a three-year period. The banks acknowledge that high turnover has been a perennial problem. The drawback is obvious: you don't want to deal with a stranger, whom you have to educate about your business (as the banks themselves effectively admit with their endless talk of "relationship banking"). Rather, you want someone who knows you, your business and your problems. That's how you build up a trusting relationship.

Ironically, the problem is worse in the commercial centres. The reason: that's where the MBA hotshots pass through on their way up the ladder. The better educated and motivated your account manager is, the more likely he or she isn't going to stick around for long. In any case, bankers have a tradition of high turnover, jumping from branch to branch, city to city, bank to bank, and bank to something else. It's explainable in part by banks' reorganizations; in part by individuals' attempts to broaden their experience, improve their salaries or use their banking experience to do something more satisfying.

A related problem is workload. Many account managers are burdened with 75 to 150 clients. In such cases, accounts that generate the greatest revenue – normally the larger accounts – are the ones that will get the attention.

The banks say they are trying to address the turnover. So they should. If a small business changed managers as often as the banks change staff, no one would lend it money.

Rejection

Rejections come in two forms – informal and formal. As many as half of banker/client meetings result in informal turndowns or in requests for further information. Formal rejections are far rarer, and some applicants are offered smaller loans than they request. The CFIB's 1994 survey found that 13.8 per cent of respondents had their most recent application for financing turned down; there were higher percentages for small or young firms. In the Western study, the top three reasons for rejection were, in order of importance, insufficient or unacceptable collateral; weak financial position or performance; and insufficient equity.

The study found that those whose applications were rejected were as upset by the manner of communication as by their failure to get a loan. They complained that the banker was abrupt or of no help in advising them on how to improve their application. Instead, bankers said such things as "Don't go into business" or "Find more collateral."[10]

If your loan proposal is rejected, find out why. Ask what you need to change to make it acceptable. "We do try and work with customers," says Warren Walker, Scotiabank's senior vice-president of commercial banking. "If he can't get it [a satisfactory answer] from the account manager, it is his privilege and his right to go to talk to the account manager's boss or even his boss until he gets a full explanation."[11]

If you think your chances of getting your branch to accept a revised proposal are poor, look elsewhere. A large percentage of rejected small business applicants are successful at another institution, often without even changing their proposal.

Ask your banker if you qualify for a business improvement loan under the Small Business Loans Act. Lending under the SBLA, which is restricted to term loans for businesses with gross revenues under $5 million, has skyrocketed. That's because of the political pressure on the banks to make more loans, and because the federal government assumes 90 per cent of any losses. The maximum interest rate is prime plus 1.75 per cent, though many banks offer better rates. There is a 2 per cent fee, amortized over the term of the loan, which is payable to the government. Personal guarantees are capped at 25 per cent, though some banks have eliminated them altogether.

Business improvement loans have been criticized for forcing the banks to make loans they wouldn't make under their normal risk criteria, and for forcing the taxpayer to pay for all but 10 per cent of any losses.

Getting advice from your banker

Most business people don't find the advice of their banker of much use, but it may be worth a try. After all, your banker is in a unique position to know what goes on in the business life of your neighbourhood. Under the Bank Act, bankers are not allowed to charge for advice, and most of them don't see themselves as advisers.

All the banks have brochures on small business, as do the CBA, all levels of government and the CFIB. The CBA runs free seminars, which are useful. It never hurts to hear from the horse's mouth what the banks are offering and what they expect in return.

Women and Small Business

Generally speaking, women have done well in small business in Canada and are responsible for more than half of all business starts. According to the Federal Business Development Bank's *Women in Business: A Collective Profile,* the number of self-employed women increased by 172 per cent between 1975 and 1990. They are particularly prominent in the retail and service sectors and generally operate newer and smaller – and hence riskier – enterprises than men.

Many small business women feel they are less well treated than men by financial institutions, and hence they are less satisfied with them. Women may have to put up more collateral and do more shopping around. Most studies, however, suggest that their problems have less to do with gender than with the type and size of businesses they run.

"The hypothesis that women business owners are particularly disadvantaged was not supported," Catherine Swift and her co-authors wrote in a 1992 study on micro-businesses. "It is clear from the analysis that the size of the firm is virtually the exclusive determinant of the interest rate which banks levy on term loans and lines of credit." The Western study reached a similar conclusion. "Some women who have experienced problems in dealing with a banker attribute these difficulties to gender bias on the part of the banks when, in fact, men share the same problems."[12]

Most of the suggestions in the CFIB's *Credit Where It's Due* make sense for both sexes.

• Since many lenders seem to be more wary of women as credit risks, women are advised to be especially well-prepared for their first encounter with a lender.

• Choose your banker carefully. Surveys have shown that women business owners put an especially high value on having an account manager with a good operating knowledge of the industry, the local market and the business owner herself.

• If you think your banker's collateral requests are excessive, do some research on what is required of businesses similar to yours, and negotiate with your banker. Bankers will, of course, press for as much collateral coverage as they can get.

• If you are running a business in a "traditional male" sector, compare the terms of credit offered to you with those offered to similar firms owned by men.

• Don't give up if you are turned down by the first or second institution you approach. Lots of people are.

• Be prepared for some resistance on lines of credit, as opposed to term loans. Counter it with a thorough business plan.

The FBDB also has a guide for women entrepreneurs, entitled *Financing a Small Business.* In a what seems sad rallying cry, it advises, "Do not be deterred by discrimination."

How Honest Should You Be?

Bankers say that total honesty and open communication are the keys to a good relationship. We should be the first to hear any bad news, they say. Since they will almost certainly hear about it sooner or later, you might as well be the one to present it, in as favourable a light as you can, and get credit for your candour.

Don't forget that the bank monitors accounts and will eventually pick up on any unfavourable trends. (Possibly sooner rather than later. "Lending officers must anticipate, not react," urges an old Bank of Montreal internal checklist of early warning signs of trouble in a commercial loan account.) "If you wait until the problems become acute, then the bank tends to pull the plug," says one commercial credit executive, "because by then it's too late to fix the problem."

Some business people, however, say that such candour is the equivalent of sticking your head in the lion's jaws. Here's the hard-headed view of Melvin Zackheim, prepared for the Canadian Organization of Small Business, on people who tell their banker their business is having difficulties: "What you have done is put the bank on notice that they had better re-evaluate and re-appraise both your business and your security which will, in most cases, result in the bank calling in your loans and/or realizing upon their security. Always look at the banker as your adversary as opposed to your ally when you are experiencing financial difficulties, and you can't go wrong."

Zackheim also warns business people not to succumb to pressure to give the bank more collateral: "You are in a better negotiating position with the bank when the amount owing to them is substantially greater than the security they hold, as once they become adequately secured, they control you."

There is no categorical answer, then, to the honesty question. It depends on your situation. Remember that you are in an ongoing, negotiating relationship with your banker. That means there is an implicit, constant struggle for advantage, however slight, as in other relationships.

It is true that when push comes to shove, the bank doesn't want to pull the plug on you and risk getting nothing. Some banks do anyway, out of inflexibility, habit, bloody-mindedness, a passion for bureaucracy or just plain stupidity. Brien Gray of the CFIB warns, "If you try to hold out on them, they will just do it to you."

According to the Western study, it takes an average of eight months for a loan to deteriorate from unsatisfactory to problem loan status, another nine months before it is called by the bank, and a further 34 until collateral is liquidated. The most frequent attempts at a solution involve restructuring the terms and pledging more collateral, assuming the borrower has more to pledge. That's why it's smart to make sure you always do.

Summary

• Get as much equity as you can before you approach a bank to negotiate debt.

• Shop around for a banker with whom you think you can establish a good, long-term relationship.

• Spend the time to prepare a thorough business plan and presentation.

• Provide as little collateral as you can get away with.

• Consider a fee package. All fees are negotiable.

• If your loan proposal is rejected, find out why. Try again.

• In most situations, it's best to be honest and forthcoming with your banker, particularly if you have built up a good relationship.

CHAPTER 5

HOW TO PAY THOUSANDS LESS FOR YOUR MORTGAGE

The Housing and Mortgage Market

Imagine you could save thousands or even tens of thousands of dollars for a few hours of concentrated work. Imagine you don't have to stop smoking, drinking or eating chocolate éclairs and don't have to draw up some dreary budget you know in your heart of hearts you will never follow. The good news is that savings on this scale are not only possible, they've been made by countless Canadians. All it takes is attention to detail and aggressive shopping at the right moment. I am of course talking about mortgages, which to many people are an afterthought to the purchase of a home, to be dealt with as quickly and painlessly as possible. The reality, however, is that some tiny type in some tiny clause in your mortgage can make all the difference between financial freedom and financial servitude for years to come.

Here's a quick example to convince you. Let's say you have a $100,000 mortgage at 10 per cent, amortized over 25 years, and pay $894.49 a month. That mortgage is going to cost you a total of $268,343, and after a quarter of a century of payments you'll be too worn down to enjoy your mortgage-free status (which brings to mind the late Enzio Ferrari's complaint that by the time most people could afford his cars, they were too old to appreciate them). Let's say you ante up an additional $57.18 a month – the price of a gourmet coffee and croissant a day – towards your mortgage. If you do, that debt-free day will arrive five years earlier and you'll save $39,942. Not enough for a Ferrari, but enough to buy a retirement sedan and have plenty left over.

Though interest rates have risen from their 30-year lows in early 1994, the market still looks relatively attractive for the home buyer and mortgage borrower. Real (inflation-adjusted) rates are high, but eventually should head back down. In any event, nominal rates have been in a broad decline since they peaked in 1981, and house prices are more affordable than they were in the mid- and late 1980s. Certainly, short-term interest rates can zigzag, because of debt, political uncertainty and a volatile dollar. But interest rates as a whole, and particularly long-term rates, ultimately respond to inflation – which reflects the level of activity in the economy – and inflation is going nowhere fast.

"Forget about inflation till about '97 or '98, at the earliest," says Lloyd Atkinson, chief economist at the Bank of Montreal and the man who predicted rates would drop as far as they did in 1992-93. "I'd never call it dead – we all know we can find an Argentinian central banker who can teach us how to create inflation. But when you look at the sluggishness in growth, central bankers almost universally committed to zero inflation, and the restructuring that has intensified competition – so that the ability of companies to pass on costs is limited – and with excess supplies and capacity in virtually every commodity category, I think people are really going to be surprised. Inflation is not going to come back any time soon."

Mortgages and houses remain more affordable than in the 1980s, when average house prices skyrocketed 265 per cent in Toronto, to $280,000 from $76,800, and by substantial but lesser amounts in Ottawa, Montreal and Vancouver. Since 1990, houses in many centres have become progressively more affordable, according to the Canada Mortgage and Housing Corporation (CMHC), which tracks the number of renters who can afford a home and the number of affordable listings. In the second half of 1993, the latest survey period, interest rates were down and house prices stable or declining. St. John's, Newfoundland, was the most affordable market, and Vancouver and Victoria were the least.

Also, thousands of Canadians have been able to buy homes as a result of federal government incentives introduced in February 1992. CMHC's First Home Loan Insurance program, which runs to 1999, allows first-time buyers, or those who haven't owned a house for five or more years, to purchase a house with a 5 per cent down payment rather than the usual 10 per cent minimum. During its first year, the program financed 12 per cent of all housing transactions in Canada, which helps to explain the activity in the lower-priced sector of the market.

Meanwhile, Revenue Canada's Home Buyers' Plan, which allows individuals to withdraw up to $20,000 each from their RRSPs to put towards the purchase of a home, is now permanent. My wife and I took advantage of the plan when it was introduced and was available to all home buyers. It has since been restricted to first-time buyers (defined as those who haven't lived in an owner-occupied home for the five years prior to using the plan). You can now contribute savings to your RRSP and put them towards a home 90 days later. Those who plan to participate should, therefore, contribute as much as they can 90 days before they plan to withdraw funds, to take advantage of their RRSP's tax-free status.

It makes sense to use the Home Buyer's Plan if it allows you to have a debt-free home before retirement, and if you take far less than the 15 years allowed to pay the money back to your RRSP. Studies show that the money saved by paying off your mortgage earlier should be invested, not spent. The plan can be advantageous to many, but remember that you are transferring money set aside for your retirement to purchase a home, and there is no guarantee that house prices will rise in the future the way they have in the past. Indeed, demographics suggest they will not – that the baby boomers fuelled the 1970s and 1980s boom in prices.

While an affordable mortgage market benefits both home buyers and home sellers, lower house prices obviously help buyers, not sellers. The flip side of lower house prices is that owners aren't able to build up equity in their homes as quickly as they did during the 1980s. Without the sense of wealth and security that comes with home equity, they will spend and risk and borrow less. And without inflation and a growing income to help them reduce their mortgage, they will carry the mortgage longer. On a more positive note, however, there will be less speculative buying and quick flips, which inevitably create markets that are begging to implode (as residents of Vancouver in the early 1980s and Toronto in the late 1980s well know).

The housing market should remain relatively slow for the remainder of the 1990s, the result of more modest economic growth and hence incomes. The slower economy will be a reflection of the drag created by high government debt levels – though the personal and corporate debt picture will be better – and by persistently high unemployment. The aging of the boomers will contribute to the slowness. As the cohort born out of the rubble of the Second World War grows older, its children will leave home. The boomers will stay put and pay off their debts, or move one final time, all the while listening to their Buffalo Springfield CDs and reminiscing about the good old days of pot and protest. If they do buy real estate, it will be cottages or land for recreational purposes.

The birth rate, inflation and house and mortgage prices will remain low, though from time to time the frequently hysterical financial markets will think galloping inflation is around the corner. Single women will buy at least as many houses as single men – they are already ahead in many major markets – with or without a partner. The phenomenon appears to be the result of women's improving incomes, the rise in the average age of marriage and the desire of many women for greater independence. A continuation of tough economic times, a lessening of pretensions and an increasing disdain for debt suggests that as many individuals will trade down to smaller, less expensive houses as trade up. Helping to keep the housing market alive will be Canada's immigrants, who traditionally start at the bottom and trade up several times, as their hard work and enterprise pay off.

Mortgage Primer
Who offers mortgages?
A mortgage is usually a loan to pay for the purchase of a property, which becomes the collateral or security for that loan.

Consumers can go to financial institutions directly or use the services of a mortgage broker, who will do their shopping for them. Brokers have traditionally been the last resort of people with poor credit; they now try to attract business for smaller lenders. Brokers are there to pursue your interests, not those of a particular institution. They do this without charge to you, collecting their fee from the bank or trust. Less happily, the reputation of some mortgage brokers leaves much to be desired. Two recent presidents of the Ontario Mortgage Brokers Association were sentenced to jail terms for fraud. Not content to steal from clients, one of them stole from his wife and parents. Thanks to this sort of enterprise, brokers in Ontario now have to disclose the full costs of a mortgage to their clients, an obligation not shared by financial institutions. They do not, however, have to disclose any referral fees they have received, so the consumer has no idea if he or she is being steered in a particular direction because it means a fat fee for the broker.

Borrowers can also turn to an Equity Centre, a chain of franchised offices across Canada acquired by FirstLine Trust in June 1993. These centres provide, without charge, overnight written mortgage offers from selected financial institutions. While the concept of having banks and trusts going head to head for your mortgage has appeal, relying upon a middleman is a poor substitute for meticulously doing the legwork yourself. At an Equity Centre, clients receive an average of three bids for their mortgage. TD is the only bank willing to pay a finder's fee to get clients; the other banks refuse to participate.

Mortgage terminology

Let's define the most common mortgage terms, and explain what they mean to you.

Amortization: The period it will take to repay the mortgage in full, and hence the length of time used to calculate your regular payments. The most common amortization period in Canada is 25 years; it is 30 years in the United States.

Term: The term is the length of time covered by your mortgage agreement. Most institutions offer terms of from six months to five years. Shorter terms became popular after the prime rate peaked in mid-1990, at 14.75 per cent, because of the widespread expectation that rates were headed down. Why lock in at high rates when you think lower rates are down the road? Conversely, why not lock in when you believe higher rates lie ahead?

The bank has an interest in lending creditworthy customers as much as it can for as long as it can. The terms that financial institutions offer are determined by what their competitors offer and by their ability to match their loans with deposits. If there's a huge demand for five-year mortgages, expect to see your bank offer very good five-year rates on GICs during RRSP season, in order to match the terms of their assets (loans) with their liabilities (deposits). Sometimes, because of a mismatch, a bank isn't keen to lend out funds with a particular term, so they don't offer a competitive rate. There are very few mortgages in Canada with terms of 10 years or more, because to offer them, financial institutions would have to offer matching deposits or securities. Given the unpredictability of interest rates, the risk of such a lengthy commitment is simply too great.

I suggested to Bank of Montreal's Tom Alton that the bank had an incentive to steer people towards longer terms. "From a client retention point of view, it's better for us if clients have longer-term mortgages," he replied. "They don't come up for renewals and people don't switch from one lender to another. But from a pure [interest rate] spread point of view, shorter-term mortgages are more profitable."

Alton produced a list of interest rate spreads showing the difference between the bank's wholesale cost of funds and the rates at which it lends – in other words, its margin. This list showed that the spread was greater for six-month and one-year mortgages than for longer terms. That, obviously, would change as the relationship between short-term and long-term interest rates changed. Of course, consumers can't know the structure of a lender's balance sheet; they can only guess what the bank wants from the interest rates offered for various terms.

As Ivan Wahl, president of aggressive, upstart FirstLine Trust, which is owned by Manulife Financial, has said, "The cost of putting a new mortgage on the books is well over one percentage point. If the borrower leaves after six months, there's just no money in it."[1]

Fixed versus variable rate: Fixed rate means the interest rate remains the same for the term of the mortgage. Variable rate means the lender can change the rate during the mortgage term, usually based on the prime rate offered by the institution. Monthly payments remain the same; it's the amortization period that lengthens or shortens when the rate changes.

Variable rate mortgages (VRMs) can be a real boon when rates are falling, or when there is a wide spread between short-term and long-term rates. When my wife and I began negotiating a three-year VRM (with the right to lock in to any term longer than six months at any time) with the Bank of Montreal in June 1992, the rate was 7.5 per cent. By the time we signed the document, the rate was 6.75 per cent. When rates skyrocketed that fall as a result of a European currency crisis (which weakened the Canadian dollar) and worries over the Charlottetown Accord, we bailed out of the VRM and signed up for a one-year open term at 8.25 per cent. A year later, after the crisis had passed, we went back to a VRM, the rate for which had fallen to 5.75 per cent. We hung on to it during the run-up in rates in the first half of 1994, since it was still the cheapest offering on the market. We were able to adjust quickly to circumstances because all our mortgages were open. It may seem like a lot of jockeying, but it saved us thousands of dollars.

Compound interest: The interest on most first mortgages is calculated, or compounded (the two words have the same meaning), "half-yearly, not in advance." The interest on most second mortgages and personal loans is calculated monthly; on credit cards, daily or monthly. The phrase "not in advance" means that you pay at the end of a month of occupancy, rather than in advance. If you rent, your February 1 rent cheque pays for

February; the same February 1 payment on a mortgage covers January.

The more often a rate is compounded, the more expensive it is. VRMs are compounded monthly. Say the quoted or "nominal" rate is 10 per cent. If the mortgage is compounded once a year, the "effective" rate, which is the rate you actually pay, is 10 per cent. If, however, it is compounded semi-annually, the effective rate rises to 10.25 per cent. If it is compounded monthly, the effective interest rate jumps to 10.47 per cent. That makes thousands of dollars of difference over the life of a mortgage.

Down payment: Under the Bank Act, the legal minimum down payment for a conventional mortgage is 25 per cent, which means the loan mustn't be greater than 75 per cent of either the sale price of the property or its appraised value, whichever is less. If you paid $210,000 for a house appraised at $200,000, the bank will lend you a maximum of $150,000. A mortgage with a lesser down payment is called a "high ratio" mortgage. Obviously, the bigger your down payment, the better, because even a small, additional sum on your mortgage turns into thousands when interest on it is compounded over many years.

Variable rate mortgages are riskier than fixed rate mortgages, of course, because the interest rate can soar overnight. That's why lenders protect themselves by demanding a minimum 30 per cent down payment on variable rate mortgages. If rates rise to the point where your payment no longer covers the interest, or your outstanding balance rises beyond 75 per cent of the value of the home, you'll hear from your bank. It may demand that you pay off the excess balance, increase your monthly payments or convert your mortgage to a fixed rate or different term.

Mortgage insurance: High-ratio mortgages must be insured by the Canada Mortgage and Housing Corporation, a Crown corporation, or by a private insurer. CMHC is charged with encouraging new home construction, administering federal housing programs and financing social housing projects. (The Mortgage Insurance Company of Canada, or MICC, the only private insurer, is winding down its mortgage business. General Electric Capital Mortgage Corp. is acquiring some of its assets.) As an alternative to mortgage insurance, borrowers can arrange a second mortgage, which will cost an extra 3 percentage points or so to reflect its greater risk. Second mortgages rank behind first mortgages in the event of default.

CMHC's mortgage insurance, which protects the lender (not you, the borrower) in case of default, has helped 2.7 million Canadians to buy homes since 1954. The fees and premiums are the same across the country. Mortgage insurance is not cheap. Premiums range from 0.5 per cent to 3 per cent of the mortgage. The cost rises with the loan's percentage of the property value; you'll pay the top rate if the mortgage loan is above 85 per cent of the value of the property. Unless you have cash, the insurance cost is added to the principal, which makes that premium very expensive over the life of the mortgage.

A second mortgage may be cheaper than obtaining mortgage insurance, but to be worthwhile it should be paid off in three or four years. Once you've paid it off, consider making the same total payments on your first mortgage, so you can pay it off more quickly.

MICC had serious misgivings about its competitor CMHC's 5 per cent down payment plan, but for competitive reasons decided to match it. The two insurers had to pay more than $1 billion in claims in the early 1980s to compensate lenders for their losses.

Closed versus open mortgages: All mortgages are closed unless the mortgage agreement states otherwise. Closed means the mortgage can be paid off in advance *only* with the lender's permission and the payment of a penalty.

A *fully* open mortgage can be prepaid any time before the mortgage comes due, without penalty or notice. You will pay 50 to 100 basis points (hundredths of a percentage point) more for this flexibility.

Some mortgages become open if you pay a penalty of three months' interest. By law, a mortgage issued for five years or more is open (there is some debate, however, over when the clock starts ticking). At the Bank of Montreal and Bank of Nova Scotia, mortgages become open after a certain period; for example, five-year mortgages are open after three years. CMHC-insured mortgages are open after the same period.

In a growing number of cases, part of the mortgage will be open and the remainder closed. Many lenders offer mortgagors (borrowers) the chance once a year to prepay 10 per cent of the mortgage (usually the original total, not the amount owing at the time). The privileges don't normally accumulate, so if you pass on your 10 per cent one year, you can't pay 20 per cent the next.

Prepayments in the early years are especially valuable because they reduce the principal on which interest will compound for the remaining years of the mortgage. Six-month open mortgages have been popular in recent years because they allow the borrower to take advantage of short-term rates, which normally are substantially lower than long-term rates, while providing an early renewal option. That allows the borrower the opportunity to lock in if rates appear to have bottomed, and the safeguard of being able to do so if they start to rise.

Since rates are volatile, the more open your mortgage is, the better. The only question is whether the premium you pay for an open mortgage is worth it.

Convertible mortgages: These give the borrower the (better) short-term closed rate, with most of the features of an open mortgage, except the ability to pay off your mortgage in full and change lenders. If the details of the conversion to a fixed rate, long-term mortgage are not in the mortgage document itself, get them in a separate letter.

Pre-approved mortgages: Getting your mortgage pre-approved makes house shopping immensely easier. You don't have to make your offer conditional upon financing. You know exactly what you can afford and, more importantly, what your bank thinks you can afford. Pre-approval doesn't obligate you to use a particular lender, but it does allow you to get a guaranteed interest rate, usually for 30 to 90 days (at least for new customers – renewing customers are often offered shorter guarantees). Pre-approval is invaluable when rates are rising and will give you a sense of certainty when they are not. Ordinarily, you will benefit if rates fall between the time you get the pre-approval and the time you negotiate the mortgage – but ask to make sure.

Competition – and How to Take Advantage of It

The bank's in a strong position when you're seeking a mortgage, but so are you. "The mentality is changing. It used to be the banks were holier than thou. It's almost as if they wanted you to genuflect in front of them. Now it's very competitive," says Toronto real estate lawyer Alan Silverstein. "Consumers are intimidated by what mortgages are all about and by banks. They don't realize that the banks need them as much as they need the banks. And because they're intimidated, they're afraid to ask a lot of questions."

Banks love mortgages. They are by far the most secure form of debt, since the penalty for delinquency can be so high – the loss of a roof over your head. Consequently, the competition for mortgages is fierce. Tom Alton, president of Bank of Montreal Mortgage Corp., estimates that losses have averaged a minuscule 3 basis points – 3/100ths of a percent – a year over the last 10 years (which means that the bank makes better returns and needs less capital to back the mortgages, under international capital adequacy rules). Mortgages are a high-volume, profitable business, and mortgage customers are the most likely to have three or four other products at the same institution.

Competition has become particularly heated because mortgage borrowing has plunged in the last five years. Even so, mortgages have become the banks' fastest growing asset, almost doubling to $148 billion in 1993, from $76 billion six years earlier. Much of the growth came through the acquisition of the mortgage portfolios of failed trust companies. The banks now have a 51 per cent share of the Canadian residential mortgage market to the trusts' 18 per cent, with the remainder divided among *caisses populaires*, co-ops, life insurance companies, pension funds and loan companies. The average bank loan for a single-family dwelling is now just shy of $100,000; in 1976 it was less than $40,000.

The banks compete for mortgages on price, features and service. They match one another quickly on price and product, sometimes on the same day. That leaves service, which – with tens of thousands of employees scattered across the country – is harder for them to deliver. If you don't get the service you want, complain, or take your business elsewhere.

Here are some tips if you're in the market for a mortgage:
• Take the time to study the mortgage alternatives carefully and to shop around. A mortgage is overwhelmingly the biggest expense in most people's lives; the interest on your loan is usually greater than the cost of your house. And, unlike in the United States, that interest normally can't be written off your taxes against other income. (There is no capital gains tax on a principal residence. The exemption on vacation and investment properties was cut in the 1992 federal budget, for real estate purchased after February 1992.) The hours of compari-

son-shopping and haggling you spend on a car purchase might save you $1,000; the same time spent on a mortgage can easily save you $50,000 in interest payments. In any case, a careful review of your income and expenditures, inevitably part of your mortgage negotiations, is always worthwhile and often a revelation.

Run for cover when you see the process reduced to something like Scotiabank's "scratch and win" mortgage contest. Or to a postcard showing a drawing of a green phone and the promise of "Loans and mortgages in under an hour, now by phone ... Don't wait, call TD Bankline." Or to "Bahamarama! Free Bahamas Vacation with Every New Mortgage" – a $1,400 value, according to National Trust's ads in the first half of 1994. Toronto-based financial planner Peter Volpé, planning to renew his mortgage, looked into it. "You had to have a mortgage for a one-year minimum term, so I couldn't take six months," said Volpé. "For the difference, I could easily afford not only to go to the Bahamas, but also to take a couple of my friends along."

• Never hesitate to ask for or even demand concessions. "Everything is negotiable," says Tom Alton. You may well get a quarter point off the posted rate simply by asking for it. The manager may be authorized to give you a half point, and in some cases more, though he or she may first have to check with head office. (This is where having a lot of business with the bank, or being willing to transfer some business, should give you clout.) All mortgage fees, which range from $75 to $350, are negotiable.

Nothing will gall the Royal more than seeing you go down the street to TD, and vice versa. Make clear you are comparison-shopping. Nonchalantly leaf through the brochure of a competitor when you talk to a bank's mortgage manager. Don't forget that different branches of the same bank can make you different offers. Whatever you do, don't start and end your search with the branch you always go to, particularly if you're there only because it's the nearest or is next door to your favourite cappuccino bar.

These days, with competition so fierce, creditworthy customers can negotiate the terms they really want. Mortgage offerings are so numerous and varied that a borrower can virtually tailor a mortgage to suit his or her needs.

• Be aware that the bank is not giving you independent advice; after all, it is trying to sell you a product. Because thousands of dollars are at stake, don't hesitate to spend a few hundred dollars to get independent advice from an accountant, real estate lawyer or reputable financial planner.

• People often get sentimental about stocks, treating them like an old friend and refusing to sell even though the company's outlook is bleak. Don't get this sentimental about your bank. Drop it like a hot potato if someone down the street offers a better deal. Many consumers are doing exactly this, a consequence of tough times and a weakening of loyalty to products and institutions. The number of "switch" mortgage applications going to the Bank of Montreal has at times approached 20 per cent of the bank's business. Over a four-year period (of rapidly declining interest rates), my wife and I had six different mortgages with three different banks on two successive houses. We saved thousands by aggressively pursuing the best deal at the best rate.

• Always do the math – or have someone do it for you – so you see exactly what you are paying in principal and interest over a year. Institutions can calculate payments differently. Some of the legislation goes back to the 1880s, something that drives real estate lawyer Alan Silverstein crazy. "When it comes to defining features and terms, there are no standards, criteria or guidelines," he told me. "Therefore, it is wide open for the banks to write their own rules." Try to talk the bank into giving you a mortgage schedule, which sets out the principal and interest payments, and the outstanding balance, or have someone with mortgage software draw one up for you.[2] That way you can see the full impact of a loan that is "front-end" loaded, which means in the early years most of your payment goes to interest. When you discover that $930 of your $1,000 payment is interest, it may encourage you to pay the mortgage off more efficiently.

• A mortgage is a legally binding document. What your bank's brochure says, or what you are told over the phone, doesn't count. Policy can change. Ensure that what you want is spelled out in the mortgage itself or in a letter. For example, the ability to "port" your mortgage to a new house is seldom put in writing, so it could be revoked. Ideally, you want a lender that offers portability alongside liberal prepayment privileges and an early renewal option.

How Big a Mortgage Can You Afford?

And how big a mortgage will the bank offer you? On this issue, at least, you and the bank have similar interests. After all, you don't want to take on an uncomfortable debt load. And the bank, of course, doesn't want you to, either.

While you may be able to afford mortgage payments at the time you negotiate, you might not be able to afford them if rates rise sharply. Get a book of mortgage payment tables and figure out exactly how much rates would have to increase before you would feel the pinch.

When you apply for a mortgage, your bank reviews your credit bureau file, your income and your debt level, then calculates your credit score. The bank may be able to see on your credit file if you've applied for a mortgage elsewhere (for example, the Bank of Montreal has begun supplying its data to the credit bureau). The credit decision will be made by your branch, unless your mortgage exceeds the branch limit, which is usually in the range of $200,000 in large cities and $120,000 in smaller centres or less expensive markets. The rejection rate is very low – about 10 per cent – and many of those rejected are accepted after they refinance some of their debt or reapply for a smaller mortgage.

A CMHC document entitled *Borrower Eligibility* is revealing. It was prepared for the guidance of lenders and is not available to consumers, which may explain the bracing tone. As it makes clear, you are well advised to be candid with your bank, because it may follow up any hints of inconsistency or any gaps in your credit record. ("File documentation is key," say the authors.) Don't, for example, try to pretend that that loan from your deadbeat Uncle Billy-Bob was actually a gift ("These gifts should be documented by a letter from the donor"). Most credit checks made by the lender go back three years. "The underwriter [of the mortgage loan] should ensure that the rationale leading to the lending decision is evident to any observer," the document observes primly.

Collateral isn't a problem as long as the bank appraises your house for an amount similar to what you paid for it. Remember, however, that bank appraisers are very conservative and are more likely to put the heat on an existing customer who is trying to refinance than on a potential new customer.

"Capacity," another of the Five Cs of Credit, is determined by two ratios. The gross debt service ratio expresses the monthly costs of your principal, interest, secondary financing (such as second mortgages or loans from relatives), property taxes, heating and 50 per cent of condominium fees as a percentage of the gross annual income of you and your partner. Most lenders say you shouldn't pay more than 30 per cent of your income to service those expenses. Let's say Bobby Bloggs makes $42,000 a year and his wife Sylvia Straightlace grosses $48,000, alongside $3,600 a year from a small consulting operation.

Husband's gross monthly income	$3,500
Wife's gross monthly income	$4,000
Other monthly income	$300
Total of above	$7,800

Maximum monthly housing payments are $7,800 x 30 per cent = $2,340. Let's say you pay $200 of this towards property taxes and $140 for heating, leaving $2,000 a month for mortgage payments.

According to a mortgage table, if the interest rate is 8.5 per cent, Bloggs and Straightlace will pay $7.96 a month for each thousand dollars of mortgage, if it is amortized over 25 years. Once we know that, we can use the following formula.

Maximum monthly payment divided by monthly payment per $1,000 of mortgage:

$$\$2,000 \div \$7.96 = \$251.26 \times 1,000 = \$251,260.$$

That's the maximum mortgage they can afford to carry. This two-income family, which grosses $93,600 a year, can afford to pay $2,340 a month for housing, including taxes and heat. If the maximum mortgage they should carry is $251,260, and they make a normal 25 per cent down payment, they can afford to buy a house for $335,013. Of course, it's prudent to borrow less than your maximum.

Our couple should also be able to meet the total debt service ratio. This includes all fixed debt obligations, from car loans to credit card debts. It's simply a way of judging whether your cash flow is sufficient to cover your mortgage payments. Here the maximum ratio is 35 to 40 per cent. If you want to be conservative, include items such as insurance costs.

Monthly car payments	$310
Average Visa card payments	$200
Bank line of credit	$160
Monthly housing payments	$2,340
Total monthly payments	$3,010

These payments represent 38.6 per cent of our couple's gross monthly income, which is just within the maximum.

As the CMHC's guidebook tartly notes, these ratios are "rule-of-thumb indicators only. An applicant's ability and desire to repay a loan is dependent to a large extent on life style and past spending habits. These should be explored if possible to ensure that the conclusions arrived at through the use of the ratios are reasonable." (This talk of exploring your lifestyle conjures up the spectre of some assistant branch manager lurking behind your privet hedge.) In other words, if you don't want to jeopardize your annual holiday in the Caribbean, be conservative.

Don't forget that you will be shelling out wads of money when you arrange your house purchase and mortgage, particularly if you are moving. There may be new appliances to buy. Expect to pay about 2 per cent of the purchase price in legal fees and disbursements.

Interest Rates

How rates are determined

When people think of mortgages, they think first of how to choose the best term with the most favourable interest rate. Let's look at how rates are determined, how they've evolved in recent times, and why they are higher than they could be – not that there's much we can do about that. Those who find this too technical can jump ahead to the next section.

Interest rates are the single most important variable in the economy and in the financial markets. More than anything else, they determine how hard it is for individuals, businesses and governments to borrow money and to repay it. As a borrower, you are concerned about the nominal interest rate, the one you are quoted by your bank or read in your newspaper. Economists and investors, however, are more interested in the "real" rate.

The real rate, which makes comparisons more meaningful, is commonly measured as the nominal rate less the rate of inflation. At the time of writing, long-term rates, as shown by the five-year mortgage rate, are 9.5 per cent. The rate of inflation, as measured by the consumer price index, is a scant 1.5 per cent. This makes for a real interest rate of 8 per cent. It's astonishing, but interest rates adjusted for inflation are higher than they were in September 1982, when five-year rates were an astronomical 17.25 per cent and inflation was 10.3 per cent (leaving real rates at 6.95 per cent). According to a Merrill Lynch economist in New York who follows Canada, they are the highest real rates in the industrialized world.

Short-term rates are also historically high. (The relationship between short and long rates is plotted on a "yield curve," the most important source of information in the bond market.) In a growing economy, long-term rates are normally higher than short-term rates. This reflects the premium paid for the risk of holding debt securities for a longer period, during which time their value can be eroded by inflation.

What determines these rates? Short-term rates are "administered," that is, manipulated – if not fully controlled – by our central bank, the Bank of Canada. Located at the head of Bank Street in Ottawa, the Bank of Canada is the agent of the federal government responsible for monetary policy. It has shown varying degrees of independence. Governor James Coyne resigned in 1961 after a famous disagreement with Conservative prime minister John Diefenbaker. John Crow was appointed in 1986 and was publicly supported by the Mulroney government in his determined and successful fight against inflation. When his term ended at the end of 1993, the Liberal government appointed the apparently more flexible Gordon Thiessen to replace him. ("No more Mr. Ice Guy," said the Globe's *Report on Business* magazine.) The governor and the finance minister have weekly meetings, and who determines policy is more a matter of practice than of theory.

Long-term rates are largely determined by the bond market. The price of bonds goes up as inflation and interest rates go down. Hence, bond traders like low inflation and the moderate or even weak economic growth that usually accompanies it. Bad news for the economy is usually good news for bondholders. The bond market is complex and the product of many forces, including the supply of bonds coming onto the market and investors' assessment of political risk (which includes the risk of not being repaid when the bonds mature).

Every Tuesday at 2 p.m., the Bank of Canada announces the results of its auction of treasury bills, which are bid on by the banks and by investment dealers, who sell them to clients. It then sets the "bank rate," which is 25 basis points, or a quarter of a percentage point, above the average yield on 90-day treasury bills. If the average yield accepted from the bidders is 6 per cent, the bank rate will be 6.25 per cent. In the preceding week, the Bank will have signalled through its activities in the money markets what rate it would like to see, so the 2 p.m. opening of the envelope isn't generally much of a surprise.

Each financial institution sets its prime rate – its base rate for lending – at a certain level above the bank rate. The banks normally raise the prime rate when the spread above the bank rate is less than one percentage point. It will be influenced not only by the current bank rate but by its view of where rates are headed. That's why when rates started to drop, the Bank of Montreal, which was certain that rates were headed much lower, led the pack in aggressively lowering its lending rates. It won the bank a lot of customers.

The strategy was initiated as a profit strategy, made possible by the shape of the bank's balance sheet; the initiative became a marketing tool only when the bank realized it could be used to gain market share. "The great surprise was our competitors let us get away with it as long as we did – for two years," Tom Alton told me with amazement. "They don't tolerate that now."

The prime rate is reserved for a bank's most creditworthy customers, most of whom are large corporations. Others pay a premium to that level. Historically, five-year mortgage rates are two percentage points higher than five-year Government of Canada bonds. The spread varies, however, depending on the volatility of rates and the eagerness of financial institutions to underwrite mortgages.

The recent evolution of interest rates

Canada's interest rates reflect rates around the globe, particularly those in the United States. Rates shot up in the 1970s, when inflation soared along with the price of oil. Inflation also explains why gold, which was $35 (U.S.) an ounce until it was deregulated in 1972, rocketed to more than $800 an ounce in 1980. Rates peaked in 1981, when the prime rate reached an astonishing 22.75 per cent in response to the double-digit inflation the country had to endure. High rates brought on a recession in 1980 and a second, more severe one in 1981-82. Unlike the recession of a decade later, it hit western Canada, with its reliance upon oil and real estate, particularly hard.

Some blame the 1981-82 recession on the six-foot-seven, cigar-chomping Paul Volcker, then chairman of the Federal Reserve Board, the U.S. Central Bank. They believe Volcker, widely considered the second most powerful man in America at the time, engineered a severe slowdown – by jacking up interest rates to punitive levels – in order to kill rampaging inflation and the psychology of inflation, which leads to the belief that prices will keep going up forever. His defenders say he defeated inflation and paved the way for the extraordinary recovery of the 1980s.

The United States and Canada began to recover in 1983, yet inflation did not come roaring back. In fact, there was some deflation – or falling prices – throughout the 1980s, with rolling recessions in energy, real estate, agriculture and many commodities. The price of gold, which is often purchased as a hedge against inflation and for that reason is seen as a harbinger of rising prices, fell over the decade, closing at the end of 1989 at $399 (U.S.) an ounce.

The same thing happened to the world's most important commodity, oil. The widely reviled National Energy Program introduced by the Liberal government in 1980 forecast an oil price of $75 (U.S.) a barrel by 1989, amid near hysteria that the planet was running out of oil. When 1989 arrived, the price was $18 a barrel, and the problem was overproduction, not lack of supply. So much for forecasts. What did shoot up in price in the 1980s were financial assets, particularly stocks, before they fell to earth with a thud on Black Monday, October 19, 1987.

To the surprise of economists, interest rates and the value of the Canadian dollar climbed in the late 1980s, even though inflation was under control and a recession was overdue, according to the pattern of past business cycles. Foreign investors liked the returns on our bonds, which they purchased with Canadian dollars, buoying both Canadian bonds and the Canadian dollar.

Economic growth in the 1990s has so far been weak, which has kept inflation subdued. The recession that began in 1990 should have given way to the traditional, robust recovery by 1992, but did not. The prices of many commodities, which are still of great importance to Canada, have been relatively weak (though lumber and natural gas are early exceptions). Oil is cheap and plentiful. Meanwhile, the commercial real estate market has collapsed, and the excess has disappeared from the residential real estate market – except in Vancouver, thanks to a relatively vibrant economy and an influx of immigrants from other parts of Canada, Hong Kong and elsewhere.

The change in psychology has been abrupt. In the early 1980s it seemed as though prices would never stop going up; a decade later, many people were wondering if some would ever stop going down – and when, if ever, businesses would stop going out of business or shrinking dramatically, throwing thousands out of work in the process.

The changes were so traumatic and profound that the Bank of Canada quietly changed its criteria for setting rates. At the beginning of the 1990s the Bank, still obsessed with its fear of inflation, bumped up rates every time the Canadian dollar weakened. A weaker dollar can be inflationary because it means Canadians pay more to buy imports, from Toyota Tercels to Boda glassware. By 1992, inflation was defeated – but so was the economy. The danger shifted from inflation to a continuation of the recession. The Bank changed gears and aggressively pursued a lower interest-rate policy, dropping rates week after week, with only the occasional, short-lived bump up when the dollar misbehaved. It began to raise rates again in early 1994 in response to higher rates in the United States and a substantial weakening of the Canadian dollar, the result of deficit worries and fears about the Quebec election and the possible disintegration of the country.

Defenders of the Bank of Canada said that governor John Crow, who was held in high esteem by foreign bankers, had fought the good and necessary fight and had successfully wrestled inflation to the ground. Critics alleged that the price had been too high, and that his high interest-rate policy – like Paul Volcker's a decade earlier in the United States – had bought on the recession and the loss of thousands of jobs. The jury is still out on the current governor, Gordon Thiessen.

Why Our Interest Rates Are Higher Than They Could Be

Canada's interest rates are much higher than they could be and are usually much higher than they are south of the border. There are several reasons for this.

First, the federal government is broke. The provincial governments, not to be outdone, have shown that they can become just as indebted. The federal government has revenues of about $130 billion a year, but spends $170 billion. The difference is the deficit. The accumulation of those deficits is our federal debt, which will soon exceed $550 billion. Before the government spends one thin dime, it has to cough up about $40 billion a year to service that burgeoning debt; this explains why the Mulroney government never made a dent in the deficit, even though it came to operate with a surplus.

Most of the annual shortfall is financed through the issue of Government of Canada bonds, a large portion of which have to be sold to foreign investors; there simply aren't enough Canadian investors to buy them. So Canada is quite literally in part owned by institutions such as Japanese insurance companies. In order to compete against other investments around the globe, we have to pay a premium in the form of higher interest rates.

Second, rates are higher than they otherwise would be because of the danger of Quebec separatism. Foreign investors worry about our constitutional crises because they drive down the value of the Canadian dollar and hence the value of any dollar-denominated investments. Big international investors see North America as a unit, and if the premium to invest in Canada isn't big enough to compensate for their worries about our deficits and Quebec, they will put their funds into the United States, which has much larger and more stable financial markets.

There is a more esoteric and controversial explanation why interest rates are so high in Canada. Banks and savings and loans in the United States fund a sizable proportion of their mortgages with mortgage-backed securities, or MBSs. Through a process known as securitization, mortgages are bundled together and sold to investors as securities – MBSs. It's been an efficient and cheap way for institutions to raise the funds needed to lend out as mortgages. Securitization is much less common in Canada. Instead, financial institutions raise the vast majority of the money they lend out from deposits and the remainder from the money markets.

One market observer has argued that Canadian mortgage rates are a full percentage point higher than they would be if the banks raised more money through securitization. He believes that they do so well from their mortgage portfolios they have no incentive to change the way they operate.[3] "There is no question that we have an oligopolistic pricing system that is keeping mortgage rates higher than they would be otherwise," says Ivan Wahl of First Line Trust, the biggest player in Canada's MBS market. "The banks are caught between a rock and a hard place. They aren't making any money from their oil and gas, commercial real estate, or leveraged buyout loan portfolios. Where are their profits going to come from if they cannibalize their mortgage portfolios?"

The argument was buttressed by a comment from a banker. "We don't feel that there is enough depth to the mortgage-backed securities market," said Phil Bergeron, then treasurer at Royal Bank Mortgage Corp. "Also, it's more profitable for us to keep the mortgages on our books."

The argument certainly touched a nerve at the Canadian Bankers Association, whose president, Helen Sinclair, responded angrily, "Competition in the mortgage lending market is alive and well in Canada."

Much of the explanation for the lack of securitization in Canada lies with the fact that Canadian banks, with their huge branch networks, can more easily raise funds from depositors than their American counterparts can. Nevertheless, the Bank of Montreal's Tom Alton concedes that "the development of the MBS has brought a competitive aspect to the industry which you have to say is healthy for the Canadian mortgage market overall."

How to Choose the Right Term and Interest Rate

Normally mild-mannered Canadians love to play the interest rate guessing game – "our form of roulette," says Alan Silverstein – an activity that frightens our usually more aggressive American neighbours. Consider the following when you are deciding on a term and interest rate.

• Interest rates are the most visible element of a mortgage, but only one of many important ingredients. Don't ignore the others. In fact, having good prepayment terms can be more advantageous than having a slightly lower interest rate.

• Be humble about your predictions. After all, many of Canada's economists are humble – or should be – after a couple of years of wrong calls on the dollar and interest rates. As with the stock market, almost no one ever calls the bottom or the top; the best most people can do is to take advantage of relatively good prices or rates and avoid relatively bad ones.

Rates are "very close to the bottom," a Royal Bank mortgage executive said in November 1991, just before they began a dramatic two-year decline.[4] But let's not be too critical about poor forecasting of something that, because of our reliance on foreign investors, is so complex and volatile. If in a wild and crazy moment the head of the central bank decided to pour his heart out to you, chances are his predictions – beyond the short term – wouldn't be that much more accurate than those of any other informed person.

• Your choice really comes down to what you can afford to pay and where you stand on the risk/reward spectrum. The more risk you are willing or able to take, the greater the potential benefits.

If you have limited equity in your home, a large mortgage relative to your financial resources and an inability to cope with a sharp rise in rates, you should probably consider a longer term mortgage. If you take a short-term mortgage, make sure it allows for early renewal so that you can lock in at the first sign of trouble to any term beyond six months, something that isn't true of all open mortgages. If you simply don't want the stress that can accompany uncertainty, you are probably better off with a longer term mortgage. First-time buyers and those with high-ratio mortgages should consider a term of three to five years.

First check to see how big a premium you will pay for the privilege of "being able to sleep at night." A difference of one or two percentage points between short- and long-term rates can translate into a difference of thousands of dollars over a few years. If the difference is huge, it's tempting to take the chance with a VRM or a six-month open mortgage, since you can lock in at any time with either. (The risk is, of course, that by the time you decide to do so, rates will already have risen.) Another way to look at the choice is to ask yourself how wrong you would have to be with a shorter term, and for how long, before you lost the rate advantage over a longer term.

My conclusion? If short-term rates are much better than long-term rates and look like they will last, and if you have the financial resources and mental toughness to withstand a sudden rise in rates, take advantage of those better rates. You should try to anticipate rather than react to rate increases, and be aware that rates often rise in advance of a crisis (such as the vote on the Charlottetown Accord), and ease after the event, even if the outcome isn't the one the markets wanted.

• The more complex offerings the banks have dreamed up may not be as attractive as they first appear.

Example 1. TD's Multi-Rate Mortgage lets you divide your mortgage into as many as five parts, each with its own term and interest rate. While the product has some appeal, it means you are locking yourself in for the long haul with one lender. The same holds true for Canada Trust's declining rate mortgage, which starts with a high interest rate and works its way down a quarter-point a year – for a full seven years. Both are big commitments.

Example 2. Royal Bank's RateCapper is a five-year, variable rate mortgage that includes a rate cap to protect borrowers in case rates shoot up. The current RateCapper rate is 8.25 per cent, with a cap of 10.5 per cent. With this plan, you pay an enormous premium for benefits you can easily get more cheaply. If you simply signed up for the bank's regular variable-rate mortgage at 6.75 per cent, you would save 150 basis points. And with the VRM you can convert to a longer term at any time without penalty. It would take a major crisis for the rate to jump 2.25 percentage points – at one point the difference was four percentage points – above 8.25 per cent and stay there for very long.

• Here's a hint for prudent borrowers with good cash flow. If you have an open six-month mortgage at 6 per cent, and the five-year rate is 8 per cent, make your payments based on the higher rate. It will prepare you for the day rates go up, if they do, and help you to pay down your mortgage faster in the meantime.

• Don't be shy; press your luck. If you ask for and receive a rate cut for a short-term mortgage, ask if you can get a similar concession (in writing) if you renew your mortgage with the same bank, or have the renewal fee waived.

• If you can anticipate how long you are likely to live in a house, try to negotiate a term of similar duration. If in three years you plan to sell the house, or expect to be transferred in your job, get a three-year mortgage so you won't have to pay a penalty to get out of a longer term. Round down rather than up, so that your term is more likely to expire a little before you leave rather than a little after. Longer terms generally have higher interest rates.

If you plan to remain a homeowner, you can get a mortgage with as long a term as you like, by booking a mortgage that is fully portable; that is, one that you can take with you (and even increase) without penalty, as long as you still meet the lender's criteria.

How to Save Thousands on Your Mortgage

You can save thousands on your mortgage through a number of simple, low-cost strategies. Nothing in your patterns of spending and consumption will ever be able to equal these savings, short of forsaking it all and heading with a tent to the nearest woods. What's remarkable is how even a little extra paid now can yield huge results over the life of a mortgage.

When you spend money on mortgage payments or on anything else, you normally do so with after-tax dollars. When you invest, you need a 20 per cent return (if you're in a 50 per cent marginal tax bracket) to net 10 per cent. By contrast, you can shield the money you save on mortgage interest by putting it into your RRSP.

Here are the best techniques to save big money. If any one of them appeals to you – all of them might – you should calculate how it will affect your situation. If you can learn from or use only one section of this book, this is it.

• Many financial institutions offer something called a "10 plus 10" (or "15 plus 15") prepayment privilege. The first 10 refers to your right to increase your regular payments by up to 10 per cent. Check to see if you can go back to the original payment schedule after you've increased the amount, just in case you find the change more onerous than you expected. You can try to coordinate an increase with your annual raise, if you are still getting one.

Let's use our $100,000 mortgage at 10 per cent with a 25-year amortization for our examples. Under the normal arrangement, you will pay $894.49 a month for 25 years, for a total interest charge of $168,343. By increasing your payments by 10 per cent, once a year from the outset, you will repay the mortgage in just under 10 years and save $99,447. You will save less if you increase your payments later in the amortization, less frequently, or by a lesser per cent.

• The second 10 refers to your right, once a year, to pay down up to 10 per cent of the mortgage balance, usually the (larger) original balance rather than the current balance. A 10 per cent annual prepayment of the original principal will reduce the 25-year amortization to seven years and result in an interest saving of $128,171.

• Most mortgages are paid monthly. However, you can also pay weekly or every two weeks (bi-weekly), though usually only for fixed rate mortgages. The idea of paying more often is so good, so simple and so painless you should ask yourself if there's any plausible reason you can't do it. Only the timing of your payments changes; everything else, including the way in which the loan is compounded, remains the same.

You save a great deal with this strategy, for two reasons. First, you pay more each year towards reducing your principal, without really noticing it. Instead of making 12 monthly payments, the equivalent of 48 weeks, you make either 52 weekly payments or 26 bi-weekly payments. That's equal to an extra monthly payment a year. Second, you reduce the principal slightly faster, because more frequent payments allow compounding to work for you.

Make sure your financial institution takes the monthly payment ($894.49) and divides it into weekly payments of $223.62 or bi-weekly payments of $447.25. If your bank instead takes the total annual payment and divides it by 52 or 26, you won't end up saving much at all. The explanation is that while you benefit from the second of the above two reasons – compounding – you don't benefit from the first and more important reason – extra payments.

If, instead of paying $894.49 a month for 25 years, you pay $223.62 a week, your mortgage will be paid off after 18 years and seven months – almost six-and-a-half years earlier – and your total interest bill will be $117,240. That's a saving of $51,103.

• Lastly, you can shorten your amortization period. When you first negotiate your mortgage, check the payments for 20 years rather than 25, the usual term. You will be surprised how inexpensive it is to cut five years off. Try to shorten the period every time you renegotiate.

Refinancing

When interest rates drop far and fast, mortgagors who have locked in at a higher rate start to fret. They see thousands of dollars in interest payments going out the door simply because they misassessed rates. It's an understandable and forgivable misjudgment, but not a cheap one. Others see higher rates down the road and want to refinance before those rates take hold. Many people, however, are horrified when they discover the penalty is thousands of dollars. The only way to decide what is best for you is to do the calculations. The frustration of those who are trapped only reminds the rest of us of the value of a fully open mortgage.

There are many reasons you might want to refinance: you sold your home; you came into some money; you're convinced rates will continue to improve; or you want to make lower monthly payments. If you have a closed mortgage, your bank can refuse to let you refinance, or can demand whatever penalty it wants. Many mortgages specify what the penalty will be. Often it's the interest rate differential or IRD (which I'll explain in a moment), or three months' interest penalty, whichever is greater. If you are near the beginning of your amortization period, three months' interest will be almost as much as three full payments.

The principle behind the IRD is fair: to compensate the lender fully (but no more) for the early termination of your legal contract. When the financial institution booked your mortgage, it matched the term and rate on the funds they were lending out with deposits, leaving themselves a profit in the form of an interest rate spread. If you break the mortgage contract, the bank or trust cannot then go back to depositors and say, "Tough luck, our borrowers have reneged and you're now going to earn less interest."

The IRD is a complex calculation, because it is not merely the difference between the old and new interest rates, but the "present value" of that sum. That's because the institution is getting its money back ahead of time in a lump sum. Let's take a personal example to illustrate. If someone had agreed to pay you $100 a month for 12 months and interest rates were 10 per cent, you would be just as well off if they handed you a cheque now for a smaller total, say $1,150, rather than paying out $1,200 over the full year.

You will need mortgage software, a discount table or your bank to calculate the IRD on your mortgage. It's lowest when the spread is slight and you are well into your term. The lender should use the current rate for the remaining term, incidentally; if you have two years left it should use the current two-year rate, not any lower rate you may have negotiated.

There will be an IRD if rates have fallen, to compensate the lender for agreeing to take less interest. The figure will be zero if rates have stayed the same. If they've gone up, in theory you should get a credit (in practice you won't), because you are doing the lender a favour by letting him out of a mortgage that has a rate below the current rate. If you are close to the end of your term, especially if you plan to stay with the same lender, you may be able to negotiate a smaller penalty or even eliminate it. If your lender is unreasonable, talk to a competitor.

Refinancing example

> Size and amortization: $100,000 mortgage,
>   25-year amortization
> Original term and rate: 5-year term,
>   12.25 per cent
> Time remaining: 2 years
> New term and rate: 2 years, 8.75 per cent
> IRD penalty: $5,852 (by comparison, the three-
>   month interest penalty would be $3,017)

When you refinance, you can figure out exactly what, if anything, you will save on the remainder of your existing term. What you can't possibly know (if you negotiate a term that's longer than the remaining term) is whether you will gain or lose, because you don't know where interest rates will be down the road. You might save $3,000 on the remainder of your existing term but lose $6,000 after that because the rate you negotiate turns out to be high. And unless you pay the IRD with cash, the penalty will be added to your mortgage balance. You will end up paying a lower rate on a larger mortgage.

Try the following test. Compare the gains you can make by paying the IRD against the advantages of using the same amount as a lump sum prepayment, for which there is no penalty. That also eliminates the possibility of making another mistake on rates.

Renewals

When your mortgage matures – when the term expires, in other words – you normally have a free hand. You can pay down or pay out your mortgage without penalty, renew with your existing lender or switch to a different lender.

Institutions often put the heat on existing customers, aware of how difficult it has been to switch. But switching is becoming much easier. Talk to the competition. They'll make it as simple as they can for you to switch, and the fees will be only slightly higher than if you were staying where you are. Do your shopping well before your term expires. See if you can get a favourable rate guarantee from a competitor for 60 to 90 days and use it as a bargaining tool with your lender. Many people do this the first time around, but don't bother for renewals, perhaps forgetting just how much money is at stake. These days you don't even have to prepare a whole new mortgage, which means you can avoid the costs of hiring a lawyer. Switching, however, is not possible in some provinces, particularly in Atlantic Canada, or if you plan to increase the size of your mortgage.

An increasing number of lenders offer an early renewal clause, available any time during the year before your term expires. It's useful because it allows you more time to choose the interest rate that you think is most favourable. The cost of this option is identical to that for other prepayments. So if your mortgage rate and the current rate are the same, you can extend your mortgage at no cost.

Summary

• You can save thousands of dollars on your mortgage. Take the job of choosing it as seriously as you do buying a house.

• Banks and trusts compete fiercely for mortgage dollars. Spend the time to see what each institution will offer you. Don't let the bank or trust company make you feel as though it's doing you a favour. Make it clear you're comparison shopping.

• Don't wait for concessions, ask for them. Begin by asking for a quarter point off the posted interest rate.

• Remember that everything is negotiable, including all fees.

• Don't hesitate to switch institutions if you're unhappy with your present one or if someone else can give you a better deal.

• Get all promises in writing. A mortgage is a legally binding document.

• Ensure that the mortgage you book is open enough to suit your needs.

• Arrange a pre-approved mortgage before you do any serious house shopping.

• Don't take on an uncomfortable debt level. In the 1980s, many people were able to handle big debts because their incomes and home equity were rising sharply. Don't count on that happening these days.

• Decide where you are on the risk/reward spectrum and choose your rate and term accordingly. Be aware of the premium you pay for the benefit of "being able to sleep at night." You achieve that benefit by locking in for a longer term at a higher rate. The short-term interest rate game has the potential to save you a lot of money.

• Save thousands by contributing an annual lump sum towards your mortgage principal, increasing your regular payments, paying more frequently, or reducing your amortization period.

• Refinance your mortgage, if it's clear from your calculations that it can save you money.

CHAPTER 6

BANK FEES AND ACCOUNTS

The Fight Over Fees

A bank charges a widow $2 to change a $20 bill for the laundromat. A child's savings for Christmas presents are decimated by bank fees by the time Christmas rolls around. A United Church minister complains that the church's account of $35 is reduced to $26 as a result of service charges. By 1988, there was a widespread feeling that Canada's banks were nickel-and-diming their customers to death, with petty charges for every possible transaction, and that it was time to take action. The best-known parliamentary committee, the finance committee, chaired by renegade Tory MP Don Blenkarn, decided to investigate bank charges. It even threatened to regulate the fees banks charged to consumers.

"I personally have thought of a number of ways of bringing banks into line," consumer advocate Madeleine Plamondon told the powerful committee. "You are probably aware of the movement in France to boycott and foul up the system. It would be very easy to pass the word to consumers. That is what we intend to do if we do not get what we want from the banks now or shortly.

"We could tell consumers to cut off the magnetic strip on a cheque and glue it to another cheque; when it goes through the sorting machine, the strip will come off and jam the machine," the president of the Shawinigan-based Consumer Aid Service (*Service d'aide au consommateur*) suggested helpfully.[1] Plamondon wanted the banks to refund the millions they had charged consumers in fees for the previous year.

Of course, nothing like this ever took place, just as no cap was ever put on interest charges on credit cards, as we have seen. How easily the banks got off, by making some modest concessions at the critical moment! Politicians searching for an easy, populist target couldn't have asked for more. They spotted a parade and decided to get in front of it. As for the United Church minister, his MP John Rodriguez read his letter to the top brass of the Royal Bank during committee hearings:

"Our church had an account of just over $35 in its balance. Unbeknownst to the treasurer – that is me – the bank started deducting $1 per month. When the treasurer finally got wise to this, the bank had milked the church account of $9 in service charges."

"You are taking money right out of God," Rodriguez thundered. "Is there no shame?" Consumers' Association of Canada president Sally Hall summarized, "Consumers tell us they are tired of feeling as if they have had their pockets picked."

The politicians were in the delicious position of being able to put the apparent culprits, including Matthew Barrett, then the president and now the much-toasted chairman of Bank of Montreal, and John Cleghorn, Royal Bank president (and chairman, as of January 1995), on the hot seat for grilling. And that's exactly where they landed. "I probably have had more complaints about your bank than the others," Blenkarn told Barrett.

The public and the committee were riled by three problems concerning bank charges. The first was lack of disclosure. Bank customers were left largely in the dark as to what charges there were, and which were going up. This made it almost impossible to shop for the best deal, in sharp contrast to the open and competitive environment on interest rates. Customers often learned about charges by seeing on their bank statement that the money had been quietly taken out of their account, the equivalent – as one observer phrased it – of discovering that you were in a no-parking zone by finding a ticket on your windshield.

Second, critics assailed the banks for the huge run-up in fee revenues, which a committee report said had risen by an average of 17 per cent a year for the five years before 1987. The banks blamed most of the rise on increased business and inflation and concluded that the real number was a relatively modest 3.3 per cent. There were widespread suspicions that the banks had upped their fees to offset their loans to the Third World, which had led to billions of dollars in write-offs.

Lastly, there was concern over the number and nature of the charges. Particular attention was reserved for the "NSF charge-back," which dinged the customer for depositing an NSF cheque, so that he or she lost twice – once on the bounced cheque and once on the charge. "This really adds insult to injury," a Royal Bank executive conceded. The other most frequent target was the "maintenance fee" for balances of less than $200, which critics said was a tax on the poor.

The banks' basic argument was that they wanted to move to a "user pay" system, in which customers paid for the services they used, and away from the system of cross-subsidization, in which low-cost, large depositors in effect subsidized high-cost customers, since the fees to everyone were the same. The banks referred to this changeover as "unbundling." They pointed out that while the trust companies had no Third World loans to shoulder, their fees were no lower than the banks'.

Some senior bankers categorically maintained they had no idea what any particular service, even one as basic as processing a cheque, actually cost the bank. That didn't prevent them from coming up with a fee. This ignorance, real or feigned, was a curiosity, since it came from banks that were among the largest and most sophisticated financial institutions in the world. If they didn't know the cost, they should have.

The blustering chief spokesperson for the banks, Robert MacIntosh, took the argument to new heights – or depths – when he told the finance committee that "I would say there is no such thing as a cost for anything you have sold." So much for Economics 101. The obvious fallacy in the argument was this: How could a "user pay" system have any meaning when the banks claimed they didn't know how much a service cost them to provide?

Put on the defensive, the banks admitted they had been overzealous on some fees, and several promised improvements. "On the pricing question, there are some irritants which we must squarely face and resolve," Matthew Barrett said. "There is the impression that prices are changed too frequently and without sufficient prior notice." He concluded his appearance before the committee by stating, "You have been told by the president of the Bank of Montreal that, if it appears reasonable that you were not informed about it [any fee], we will reverse the charge."

The issue came to a boil in June 1988, when the spectre of government regulation raised its head. The parliamentary committee tabled a report and a bill, supported by all three parties on the committee, that would have forced the banks to eliminate certain service charges. Ironically, this threatened not only the banks but also the Conservative government of Brian Mulroney, which was committed to a free-market philosophy and in particular to financial deregulation. The Toronto-Dominion Bank, which was the least willing to budge on any issue, said it was "astounded, incredibly angry and frustrated" with the report.

The Outcome

After private negotiations with the government, the banks and federally regulated trust companies agreed to further concessions, some of which, particularly in the area of disclosure, were introduced as amendments to the Bank Act. The banks acted because it was clear that if they didn't do something to satisfy public opinion, the government would do it for them. Consumer and Corporate Affairs Minister Harvie Andre had written a warning letter to them in the spring, and fired a shot across the bow when he said in an interview, "It would be prudent on the part of banks and others to act before action is imposed upon them."

The banks – with a couple of exceptions on a few items – agreed to change their fees only once a year; to give at least 60 days' notice of increases through signs in branches and send out 30 days' notice of same with account statement mailings; and to get rid of the charges that had caused the most complaints. They included the NSF charge-back and a fee to close an account after 90 days. They also agreed to make available no-frills accounts with no charges for withdrawals. Realistically, this is the most that bank customers could have hoped for. Not even the Consumers' Association had supported government regulation of fees.

There is no evidence that the banks increased their fees to compensate for disastrous loans to Mexico, Brazil and other Third World countries. But it is clear that those loans, and international lending in general, produced a shortfall in profits and led to a search for new sources of earnings.

There were other important forces at work. Computers had made possible the calculation of daily interest, and more and more Canadians were taking advantage of it and the higher rates paid to depositors. This meant that the banks were making less than they had in the past on interest rate spreads, that is, the difference between what they pay to depositors and what they charge on loans.

As problems continued on the international scene, Canada's chartered banks faced far stiffer competition domestically, thanks to aggressive policies on the part of foreign banks and powerful trust companies such as Royal Trust, Central Guaranty Trust and Canada Trust (the first two have since disappeared as independent operations). Consumers were increasingly using banks for transactions – such as paying bills and writing cheques – that left the banks with slim profit margins, while putting most of their funds in trust company savings accounts. The banks were missing out on cheap deposit funds while getting stuck with expensive, labour-intensive transactions.

Pressed in the late 1980s by competition to increase interest rates on deposits, the banks began charging more and bigger fees to increase earnings. Since the fees weren't well advertised, or – by the banks' own admission – based on cost, institutions didn't compete on them. That left them to charge whatever they thought the market would bear.

Where We Stand Today

Federal politicians have not looked at bank charges since 1988. Fast forward to 1994. There has been progress, and some backsliding. Some of the banks still have NSF charge-backs. Disclosure has vastly improved, with each bank producing brochures itemizing its charges (however, the attempt to get all the banks to list their fees at each ABM failed). Better disclosure has made comparisons between banks easier and led to greater competition.

That competition, and suggestions that consumers and small business customers would be forced to carry the can for the demise of the Reichmanns' real estate empire and the huge loan losses that went with it, led most of the banks to freeze their fees in July 1992. In the 1980s critics said the banks increased fees to compensate for Third World losses; in the 1990s the banks disarmed critics by decreasing fees when a crisis broke. Some of the freezes on listed fees have ended; Bank of Montreal's, however, remain frozen to the end of 1994, and Royal Bank's till May 1995.

In 1988, Don Blenkarn asked Bank of Montreal's Matthew Barrett what service he supplied "the poor bugger" who was charged a $1 monthly maintenance fee for keeping his money in an investment savings account, if the balance fell below $200. "You still think you are entitled to charge people to put their money in your account," Blenkarn roared. Barrett acknowledged the issue generated more complaints than any other and said no maintenance fee would be charged on a basic savings account. Though discontinued on Bank of Montreal's basic savings and chequing accounts, that monthly fee for balances under $200 has continued on investment savings and investment chequing accounts.

The banks were smart to compromise in the late 1980s. Since then, the issue has largely disappeared from the public agenda. Bank focus groups reveal that consumers are much more concerned about service, or the lack of it. Thanks to the efforts and profile of Blenkarn and his committee, which included some remarkably well-informed MPs, awareness of the fee issue has increased. Consumers realize there are fees for just about everything, and the banks realize there are limits to what they can charge. The average bank customer is probably paying $120 to $140 a year in fees, though it's hard to generalize. Fee increases and larger volumes of business have translated into much greater fee income for the banks. Fee income in all categories at the Bank of Montreal, for example, was $1.58 billion in 1993, 60 per cent more than in 1989.

The problem for bank customers now is the bewildering variety of fees, the accounts to which they apply, and the difficulty in making sense of them. The hapless customer is left with as many as 150 to 200 different products at a single institution. This smorgasbord is reminiscent of the days when car buyers had a similar, meaningless variety of models and sub-models of Detroit iron from which to choose.

There is also an apparent irrationality to many of the fees, with a $1 charge for a service on one account and a 50-cent charge for exactly the same service on a different account. The same holds true for accounts. At the time of writing, Scotiabank's daily interest chequing account offers a higher interest rate than its basic savings account, something even the bank finds inexplicable.

Here's a partial list of the charges that you, the customer – not to mention that poorly trained and underpaid customer service rep behind the bank counter – have to keep up to date on: fees for rolling and unrolling coins, with fees schedules carefully distinguishing between uncounted and counted rolls; for post-dated deposits; for stop payments; for transfers of funds between accounts; for transfer confirmations; for a wire transfer investigation of a non-bank error; for U.S.-dollar cheques drawn on, or deposited into, a Canadian-dollar account; for closing an account within 90 days of opening it; for certification of your balance; for a duplicate statement; for notice of an unclaimed or inactive balance; for using cheques without preprinted account numbers; for an account balance transfer to another financial institution; for the depositing or supplying of rolls of coins; for searches of accounts and old records and credit reports (which in most provinces you can get free directly from the credit bureau). Expect to pay $30 to $40 an hour for staff time, if they have to track down documents that you have requested.

The banks have also long considered even charging fees for deposits, but no one has been bold enough – or foolish enough, because deposits are the lifeblood of the system – to do so.

Deposits, after all, are the main source of cheap funds for the banks, and the number-one reason for their strength.

"It's frankly a disaster out there, in terms of the complex product offerings and the pricing structure and the apparent inconsistent application of the prices against those products," admits John Kearns, CIBC's senior vice-president, savings and investments. "Our own staff were having difficulty dealing with it." CIBC is simplifying its offerings, which have included nine different accounts.

Why do banks have so many product offerings and so many fees? One view is that, in a highly competitive environment, the banks are constantly on the lookout for new, low-cost, high-value niches they can fill to satisfy existing customers and attract new ones. A less happy view – held by Robert Kerton, a University of Waterloo economics professor and adviser to the Consumers' Association – is that, when the members of an oligopoly compete, they create so much "noise" – in this case, a confusing diversity of products – that consumers can't find bargains, and high prices can continue.

Let's look first at choosing your accounts, and then turn to the question of how you can save money on fees on those accounts and on other services.

How to Choose an Account

Choosing the right account or accounts does matter. Canadians forgo tens of millions of dollars' worth of interest every year by putting their money in the wrong accounts. Ask your branch for advice on both accounts and fees. You never know, they just might have some good ideas.

You must first decide whether you want separate institutions for your deposits and your borrowing. One institution for both is more convenient and should give you more clout. Be aware, however, that if you are overdue on your credit card or on some other payment, the bank has the legal right (through the common law Right of Offset) to take whatever is owed out of your account. It obviously can't do that if your savings are with a separate institution.

Pure savings accounts pay interest, but cheques cannot be drawn on them. Pure chequing accounts allow chequing, but pay no interest. They have lower fees to make up for the lack of interest. There are myriad, hybrid chequing/savings accounts, which allow chequing and pay nominal interest.

Most people will want to keep a minimum balance in a chequing (or perhaps a chequing/savings) account to pay bills. Obviously, there's no point in putting savings in the account because you will earn little or no interest. At the same time, you should keep the balance above whatever minimum the bank has set – often $1,000 – to reduce fees on cheques and withdrawals. You cannot go below that $1,000 level for a nanosecond during the month, or the fee bell will start ringing.

Your savings can go into a savings account, into what the banks call investment or T-bill accounts, into a money market fund or into treasury bills. (The bank account will be more convenient, because it allows withdrawals, while treasury bills will probably offer a higher interest rate.) Check to see if your institution offers a chequing money market fund.

Keep your savings account balance above whatever minimum has been set to earn interest. You can transfer money out of the account and into your chequing account as required, keeping in mind that you may pay a hefty transfer fee if you make your request by telephone or mail. If you are paying a fee for transfers or withdrawals, make them larger and less frequent to lessen the charges.

Many people have two or three savings accounts at different financial institutions. You might be wiser to consolidate savings accounts to ensure that your balance remains above any minimum required to earn interest, and to take advantage of the higher rates that are paid for larger balances in "tiered" accounts. Note that you might earn 5 per cent interest on a daily closing balance of $25,000 to $59,999, and 6 per cent on $60,000 to $100,000. That 6 per cent probably applies only to the portion above $60,000, not to the entire balance – a point you should clarify. Don't consolidate your accounts if it puts you above the $60,000 limit per institution on deposit insurance, discussed below.

Remember there is always a trade-off between the fees you pay and the interest you earn. If you had $1,000, which account would make more sense – a no-fee, no-interest chequing account or a chequing/savings account that paid 3.5 per cent a year in interest but cost you $30 in fees? And the winner is... the no-fee, no-interest account, even though it yields nothing. The $30 in fees on the second account outweighs the $35 it earns in interest. Why? Because the fees come out of after-tax income while the interest is subject to tax. If your marginal tax rate is 44.4 per cent (the rate for someone with a mid-range income), you are left with only $19.46 of that $35 in interest after the tax bite.

As discussed earlier, the nominal or posted interest rate and the effective interest rate are not the same thing. The more often interest compounds, the more money you will make. When you are choosing an account, ask your banker to compare effective, not nominal, rates for you.

If you are under 18, a college or university student, or more than 60 years old (some institutions have plans for customers as young as 55), your bank will probably offer you an attractive deal on accounts and fees. It may in fact charge you no fees. Institutions want to attract the young, hoping to turn them into lifetime customers, and the old, because many of them have substantial assets and tend to pay what they owe. If you are in this older age category and your spouse, whatever his or her age, has an account with the same bank, he or she might qualify for the same benefits. Make sure you apply for these benefits. Otherwise, the banks will charge you what they charge everyone else.

A joint account makes sense for joint household expenses, assuming you can trust your spouse or partner not to abscond with the funds.

If you travel frequently or take long holidays in the United States, or if you get income from the United States or do a lot of buying there, a U.S. dollar account might make sense. Those who have them have a good customer profile (read: tend to be affluent), so many institutions offer attractive packages, including free money orders and travellers' cheques. Some banks even mail statements to U.S. addresses. There are, however, two disadvantages to U.S. dollar accounts: they are not covered by deposit insurance, and you cannot get access to them from an ABM.

These accounts generally offer low rates of interest. To decide whether one of these accounts suits you, weigh the interest you forgo against your savings on currency conversion. Say you can get 2 per cent interest on a U.S.-dollar account instead of 4 per cent from a Canadian-dollar account, but save 2 per cent on transaction charges. You are way ahead of the game, because your interest is taxed while your savings are not.

Bear in mind that there is also a hidden cost in converting from one currency to another. Suppose you are going on holiday to New Orleans and convert $3,000 Canadian into U.S.-dollar travellers' cheques. You spend only $2,200. Unless you convert the cheques back to Canadian dollars – which means a second set of charges – you will have $800 in cheques sitting around the house earning nothing, waiting for your next escapade south of the border. That hidden expense won't occur if you use your

U.S.-dollar account to pay for your holiday.

A final word about all accounts that earn interest. In 1988, the federal government ruled that financial institutions must ask customers to supply a social insurance number when they open interest-producing accounts, though they can open them without a SIN. Revenue Canada doesn't want to miss out on any tax dollars it is owed. If you don't provide your SIN, it is the tax department, not the bank, that could come after you.

How to Save Money on Fees

Decide what you need

Begin by figuring out what services you need, and what you are now paying for services. Flip through a year's worth of statements and come up with a total. If your statements are anything like mine, it will be tough to know why you paid what you did. I see a lot of "SCs" for service charges, but no indication of what they are for. Ask your branch to help you, and get a copy of your bank's fee schedule so you know what services they charge for. This exercise alone can easily save you $100.

How do you like to pay your bills? If you are disciplined with your credit card and never carry balances, using a card with no transaction charge is a lot cheaper than writing cheques, which can cost 50 or 60 cents a pop, or paying withdrawal or debit card charges. And the card's grace period gives you interest-free credit.

Consider a package

The "unbundling" process of the late 1980s has been replaced by "rebundling," with all institutions offering service plans. Decide if one would save you money. Is there a plan that includes the services you actually want (such as the use of another institution's ABMs, which normally costs $1)? Or are the packages padded out with items you seldom use, like a discounted rate on a safety deposit box or free cheque certification? Standard packages cost around $9 or $10 a month ($108 to $120 a year), which is a lot of cheques and withdrawals at 50 or 60 cents a hit. However, you might get a discount if your monthly balances are high enough. If you do go for a package, there may also be a deal for your spouse, if he or she uses the same bank.

Try telephone banking

"If you can order pizza, you can bank by phone," suggests TD's brochure. Okay, I can do that. And if you give TD's brochure, or that of its competitors, a look, there will probably be a demo number you can use to try it out. That's exactly what I did. The one disadvantage? After a while, that nagging, disembodied, monotone voice will start drilling through the back of your head.

Telephone banking is convenient, since it allows you to do at least some of your banking – generally paying bills, transferring money between accounts and confirming transactions and balances – when you want, from your home or office. Transactions are immediate and are therefore easier to keep track of. You can make post-dated bill payments. You can pay bills from your holiday hotel room in New Mexico. Charges are the same as or less than regular charges, though there is likely to be a monthly fee. Once again, if you've signed on, your spouse could be eligible for preferred rates.

Computer banking – which so far is available only for small business – is also becoming available for computer geeks. At this stage, it's expensive – TD charges $45 a month for one service that has a limited number of functions, which include accessing information and transferring money between accounts. You can also go on line with TD Green Line, the bank's discount brokerage operation, to buy and sell stocks. Presumably, by the time this book is growing musty, no one will have visited the branch of a bank in years, preferring to conduct all of their banking business by phone or computer. The first big change will occur when you are able to get cash at home through a "swipe" transaction, similar to that for a debit card.

Use an ABM

Use automatic banking machines as often as you can for transactions – especially to pay your bills, for which no fee is usually charged (it costs about $1.25 to pay a bill through a teller). There are lots of machines to choose from: Canada has more of them per capita – 5.3 per 10,000 inhabitants – than any of its industrial competitors except Japan. It will take a couple of days for bills you pay at an ABM to be credited to your account. Remember to keep confidential your PIN, which only the computer – not even your bank – will recognize.

ABMs are high on the list of complaints made to banks. Here's one of the most common. You have $200 in your account but need $500 over the weekend. You deposit a cheque for $500 into the machine and then try to withdraw $500. You can't! It will only give you $200, because – for all the bank knows – your deposit envelope was empty (a frequent scam in the United States). The banks are trying to address this problem, and some offer a plan to get around it. Scotiabank, for example, has a "Cashback" service that allows depositors to withdraw up to $1,000 after depositing a cheque.

Incidentally, because there are now all those ABMs out there groaning with $20 bills, the cost to the banks of armoured car services has skyrocketed.

Pre-authorize

It makes sense to pre-authorize for fixed payments, such as your mortgage and car insurance. It will ensure that you do pay and allow you to pay on the due date. Similarly, arrange to have regular payment cheques, such as your salary or pension, deposited directly, so that you start earning interest right away.

Other tips:
• Get overdraft protection, if you are in the habit of bouncing cheques.
• Save money by using money orders and bank drafts instead of certified cheques.
• Avoid counter cheques, which lack bank coding. They carry a large fee because they have to be processed manually.
• Keep track of all your accounts and those of your partner. For a search of the accounts of deceased or incapacitated individuals, CIBC charges $6.50 per name per branch, with a $22 minimum, plus GST.
• The bank will usually place a hold on a cheque you deposit if it isn't familiar with the individual or company that gave it to you, or if you are new to the bank. The hold is usually for seven business days – more if it's drawn on a foreign account. When in doubt, ask the teller when the funds will be released. If you need the money sooner, say so.
• There are limits on the amount you can withdraw when you're away from your branch. The bank can demand up to 30 days' notice of withdrawals, though they seldom invoke the right.
• Protest any fees you were unaware of or that seem exorbitant. The main branch of Bank of Montreal in Ottawa once tried to charge me hundreds of dollars for a search of old records, which they said had been moved to Montreal. I protested, and we agreed on $100.
• Check your statement when you receive it. You normally have 30 days to dispute any items.

Manna From Heaven: Dead Accounts

Don Gould, Doug Goold, what's the difference? Maybe the TD Bank won't notice, and I'll be able to claim the $1,480 unclaimed balance that Don has left sitting in an account since 1982.

I don't know who Don Gould is, and his address is unknown. But the $1,480 he was to be paid by the city of Kingston, Ontario, more than a decade ago, is duly noted in the *Chartered Banks Unclaimed Balances* supplement to the *Canada Gazette*, the official voice of the federal government published every June. To find out if any of the unclaimed $116 million is owed to you, your relatives, neighbours, friends or enemies, head for the nearest library. The Bank of Canada, which you can write or phone, will do a free record search.

The *Gazette* is surprisingly entertaining reading. Did these thousands of people fall off the earth, are they deceased, or are some of them just really disorganized? How could Shearson Loeb Rhodes of Calgary, who sounds for all the world like an investment firm, have forgotten about $67,840.75 in 1983? How could Margaret Wilson, whose 1983 street address in Calgary is given, or her heirs, forget about $37,000? And what about this guy "Inconnu," who is owed so much money?

Maybe these grand, unclaimed sums are the result of the proliferation of accounts, and the tendency of some people to move from place to place. After many summers in England and three years completing a doctorate at Cambridge, I had opened (but failed to close) eight accounts, divided between Cambridge and several addresses in London, between chequing and savings, between former lives and current lives.

The *Gazette* lists amounts of $100 or greater that have remained unclaimed for nine years or more and that have been passed on by the banks to the central bank, the Bank of Canada. If you spot your name, contact the branch of the bank in question.

You have to hope that the bank still has the old records, and that you are able to back up your claim. If the branch with its stylish Corinthian columns is now a McDonald's parking lot, write the head office of the bank.

Banks charge hefty fees for inactive accounts. Expect to pay $30 for an account that has been dormant for five years. You may also face a search fee for documents.

Unless you are unhappy with your bank, don't switch institutions when you move. That way you will eliminate the possibility of losing track of your old accounts and of spreading your assets too thin, which could mean higher fees. And a few things, such as preauthorized deposits and payments, are hard to move. Your bank will be only too happy to help you transfer your business to a different branch.

Deposit Insurance

Few people, even well-informed investors, know exactly what is and what is not covered by federally backed deposit insurance. How about that Canadian dollar account in the Cayman Islands – surely that's covered? No? Well, what is?

Let's start with what isn't. The Canada Deposit Insurance Corporation, which crowbars its money – though not enough to cover its liabilities – out of the financial institutions that belong to it, does not insure U.S.-dollar accounts, or those of any other non-Canadian currency. It does not insure stocks, bonds or investments in mortgages or mutual funds, including money market funds.

It limits its coverage for individual depositors to $60,000 per member institution (not per branch) of Canadian-dollar-denominated deposits, payable in Canada. Eligible deposits include savings and chequing accounts, term deposits (including GICs and loan company debentures), money orders, drafts, certified drafts and cheques, and travellers' cheques issued by members. The deposit must be payable within five years, so a six-year GIC is not insured, not even for its first five years. Nor are treasury bills, though they are effectively without risk because they are issued by the federal government.

All banks, trust companies and loan companies are required to be CDIC members. Most members display the CDIC sign, a take on the Canadian flag, on their front door, and make available the corporation's brochure. If you have any questions, phone them in Ottawa at 1-800-461-CDIC. Deposits made in Quebec with provincially regulated members are protected by the Quebec Deposit Insurance Board. Ask your credit union or *caisse populaire* about its deposit insurance, which varies by province.

The $60,000 includes accrued interest, so if you have a $55,000 GIC at 10 per cent (good on you, if you do), you will be over the limit before the year is up, and the excess amount will not be covered.

You can increase your limit by a further $60,000 for each of the following:
• Jointly held deposits.
• Trust deposits, whereby you are a trustee for someone else.
• Deposits held in RRSPs, so long as they meet the same criteria (payable in Canadian currency, etc.) as those above.
• Deposits held in RRIFs, as long as they meet the same criteria.
• A deposit in an institution that is separate from but related to an institution in which the depositor also has an insured account (e.g., Scotia Mortgage Corporation, a subsidiary of Bank of Nova Scotia).

The examples provided by the CDIC show you could technically have insured deposits of $240,000, not $60,000; your partner could have the same amount, and you could top it up with

$60,000 of coverage of joint deposits. Grand total: $540,000.

The CDIC has taken a mega-bath in recent years, as one trust company after another has folded, and customers' hands have been outstretched to receive compensation. A controversial new study by the C.D. Howe Institute argues that it is no coincidence that there were no bank failures between the suspension of the Home Bank in 1923 and 1966, the year before the CDIC was established, while there were 30 bank and trust failures between 1967 and 1992.

"Deposit insurance is used to provide a subsidy to politically important high-risk and regionally concentrated deposit-taking institutions," argues the University of Toronto's Jack Carr and his co-authors, pointing to the establishment (and demise) of institutions such as the Alberta-based Canadian Commercial Bank and the Northland Bank. By providing depositors with 100 per cent insurance against loss, the CDIC has encouraged these depositors and institutions to take big risks to get greater returns.

"Deposit insurance has reduced market discipline on management and increased the returns to imprudence and fraud," they write. "[It] has ensured higher rates of failure among banks, trust and mortgage loan companies, and reduced the stability of the financial system."[2]

More responsible institutions and their depositors were left to pick up the tab. As a result of the failure of Central Guaranty, First City, Standard Trust, Principal Savings & Trust, Northwest Trust, Bank of British Columbia, Northland Bank and Pioneer Trust, the CDIC has paid out $3.6 billion as of the end of 1992, which has left it $1.65 billion in the hole. As a result, premiums charged to CDIC members have been going up. The solution to this unhappy state of affairs could be some form of co-insurance, whereby depositors assumed a share of the risk.

Summary of Tips

• Ask your branch to help you choose the accounts that best serve your needs.

• Keep at least a minimum balance in your accounts, to maximize interest and minimize fees.

• Consolidate your bank accounts. You probably need two, not six.

• Add up the fees you are paying, and determine if a package plan would help you to save.

• Use an ABM as often as you can, particularly for paying bills.

• Ensure that your deposits are covered by the Canada Deposit Insurance Corporation.

I think most Canadians
are very smart about their money.
A small percentage are not very smart,
and most of them either work
for newspapers or write to newspapers.

ROBERT MACINTOSH, FORMER PRESIDENT,
CANADIAN BANKERS ASSOCIATION

This year's champ
is next year's chump.

ROBERT POWELL, EDITOR,
MUTUAL FUND MARKET NEWS. BOSTON.

CHAPTER 7

MUTUAL FUNDS AND GICS

The Evolution of Mutual Funds

For decades, what the banks did was pretty straightforward. They raised funds by paying depositors for their savings. Then – acting as an intermediary – they lent the money back to those depositors, and to others, at a higher rate. The spread between the two rates allowed them to cover their expenses and to make a profit.

Demographics and amendments to the law changed this sleepy, predictable formula. First, Canadians, led by the aging baby boomers, started to spend less and save and invest more. (Canadians traditionally save at least twice as much – as a percentage of their disposable incomes – as Americans.) As the work force grew older, and as it accumulated money from real estate and from inheritance, it looked towards retirement. Aware that government pension plans might be underfunded by the time they would be needed, the boomers turned away from low-yielding deposit accounts and towards more profitable investments, particularly mutual funds. Mutual funds are professionally managed investment pools.

The spectacular performance in recent years of funds such as those of Altamira Investment Services, whose high-profile equity fund regularly produced annual returns above 30 per cent, attracted the savings of hundreds of thousands of Canadians.

At the same time, more people were becoming financially literate and hence more comfortable with higher risk, higher return investments. By 1992-93, as interest rates headed towards 30-year lows, traditional deposit accounts were offering what many considered to be unacceptably low returns. Those accustomed to 10 per cent returns on guaranteed income certificates (GICs) or other fixed-income products were unwilling to accept half that rate and looked for new homes for their investment dollars.

As money flowed into stocks, bonds and mutual funds, and away from deposits, the banks and trust companies were left with a difficult choice. They could either watch their traditional deposit bases erode, or adjust to the changing environment and get in on the action. Not surprisingly, they decided to get in on the action.

This became possible after changes to the Bank Act. Under the Act of 1979, banks were restricted to selling mortgage funds. That restriction was lifted in 1987, and they were allowed to sell funds of all kinds.

The Spectacular Growth of Funds

The results of this amendment – and of the consequent shift in savings patterns – have been dramatic. In 1987, Canadians owned $20 billion worth of mutual funds. By the spring of 1994, they owned $132 billion. In 1987, banks and trusts had 15 per cent of total fund assets, with trusts well ahead of the banks. By early 1994, they had a combined share of 36 per cent. Banks had almost triple the trust company share, a reflection of their ownership of many formerly independent trusts.

Winnipeg-based Investors Group, the only independent mutual fund company with its own sales force, holds down the top spot, with assets of $16.3 billion. Investors is owned by Paul Desmarais' Power Corp. of Montreal. The Royal Bank, with its takeover of Royal Trust, has replaced Mackenzie Financial in second place (Royal Bank/Royal Trust set an industry record by selling almost

$1 billion in funds in a single month, January 1994). Next on the top 10 list of mutual fund companies are Trimark, CIBC and TD. Not a bad showing for the banks, given how little time they have fully been in such a fiercely competitive business.

The largest of the more than 700 funds available to Canadians is the Investors Mortgage Fund, with assets of $3.6 billion, followed by Bank of Montreal's First Canadian Mortgage Fund. Seven of the top 15 funds are bank funds; all of these are in lower-risk mutual fund categories such as money market and mortgage funds.

Mark Maxwell of Gordon Capital predicts that by the year 2000, mutual funds' assets will equal personal bank deposits at $300 billion (deposits are now almost three times the size of mutual fund assets). This is a less daring prediction than it appears. The American funds industry is 20 times the size of Canada's – double what the relative populations would suggest – and presumably we will close much, if not all, of the gap. American fund assets already surpass American deposits.

Fewer women than men own mutual funds. Women prefer more conservative investments such as GICs, and a smaller percentage of them say they understand how funds work. The co-author of *Everywoman's Money Book*, Betty Jane Wylie, suggests that while "women see money as a security blanket, men see it as a power tool."[1]

The rapid growth of the banks' mutual fund assets has come at a price. To some extent, they have cannibalized their own deposit bases, in effect encouraging their customers to withdraw funds from deposit accounts and GICs in order to put them in mutual funds. As one analyst has phrased it, the banks risk giving up a business that has a 3 per cent interest rate spread for one that offers a 2 per cent fee. Because bank mutual funds do not have initial sales charges (front-end loads) or charges when funds are redeemed (rear-end loads), customers have little incentive to hold on to these funds during a financial crisis.

Despite these potential problems, the banks' funds will likely continue to grow. In fact, the banks will probably eventually be forced to offer the funds of their non-bank competitors, alongside their own. The banks realize that changes in the demographics of the Canadian population and in savings patterns are long-term, so the sooner they adjust to them the better. Besides, while deposits by law must be backed by the banks' own capital, mutual funds have no capital requirements.

The banks' move into mutual funds is just another part of the breakdown of the traditional barriers among the four pillars of the financial services industry – the banks, trusts, insurance companies and investment dealers. Federal legislation in 1992 allowed each of the four to move into areas traditionally reserved for the others. (There are still restrictions, however. For example, the banks are still not allowed to sell insurance through their branches, the result of an intense lobbying effort by the insurance industry.) The goal of those who make up each of the pillars of the financial services industry is to get the customer in the door and offer him or her "one-stop financial shopping," with a view to getting as large as possible a percentage of that individual's assets under management.

In a 1993 report, Gordon Capital's Mark Maxwell declared the four-pillars model obsolete. With more than $300 billion in pension assets, and billions in both private client assets and in mutual funds, a fifth pillar – investment management – has grown up. With their increasing interest in trust accounts and financial planning, the banks have been aggressively pursuing the business associated with that fifth pillar. Their ownership of Bay Street investment dealers and their takeover of trust companies has already left them with a huge amount of control over two of the three other pillars.

Why Are Funds So Popular?

What explains the phenomenal growth of funds, and of bank funds in particular? Canadians have come to see the advantages that mutual funds present: diversification, professional management, and – if you choose right – performance (although, until the big run-up in 1993, Canadian equity funds, the largest category, for years underperformed the Toronto Stock Exchange, which itself underperformed all of the world's major markets). The early 1990s, the period of greatest growth in funds, coincided with vigorous stock and bond markets and falling interest rates; this in turn produced "GIC refugees," who left their normal haven in favour of funds. As many as two-thirds of new fund buyers were buyers by default.

Banks aided the transition to funds by putting their imprimatur on the process, thereby giving it respectability. They had several important advantages, which together explain the growth of their market share. First, they had a vast, captive clientele, and branches across the country to serve it. Second, they were able to take advantage of the powerful trend towards no-load funds, by offering only no-load funds themselves. Lastly, they had plenty of money for advertising and marketing. That's particularly critical in the days leading up to the last day of February, the RRSP deadline, when there are hundreds of funds competing for the attention of harried RRSP shoppers. The banks can get your attention, either through ads in the media or in branches, and then lend you money at prime to buy their funds. They also make it easy to transfer money from your account to your funds on a regular basis.

This rush into mutual funds has produced a growing unease in some quarters. Novice investors, with little knowledge of what their funds contained and no real understanding of the risks, poured millions into funds that invested in countries they would be lucky to locate on a map. "Get ready for the mutual fund crash," Patrick McKeough warned in *Investor's Digest* in December 1993, pointing out that only six of the top 20 American funds from the "go-go" era of the 1960s are still in business.

Do investors in Altamira's hot equity fund really want to rely for their retirement upon something as uncertain as the mining prospects of Venezuelan Goldfields (renamed Vengold), and its promoter, Vancouver-based Robert Friedland, best known for the now bankrupt Galactic Resources? (It's been one of the fund's most successful holdings to date.) While the fund has been brilliantly managed by Frank Mersch, it does involve risks. However impressive its performance, prudent investors should diversify beyond it.

Meanwhile, I wrote a column for *The Globe and Mail* entitled "Sell?! To whom? managers' dilemma," in which I argued that fund managers would have no one to whom to sell their stocks (particularly smaller, thinly traded ones) if the market started to fall and panicky, novice investors ran for the exits. Fund managers can pay for redemptions in only two ways: either by having cash on hand (which creates its own problems, because it is uninvested) or by selling securities. If the market started to slide, they would be forced to sell them at the worst possible time.[2]

The banks are particularly vulnerable – not that anyone expects a problem soon. With no load, there is no commitment on the part of the investor, who can get out of the fund as easily as he or she got in. With no advice or hand holding, there is no development of reasonable expectations. Hence the banks could face a redemption problem, particularly on higher risk, high-volatility funds, such as Far East funds, which can go up 80 per cent one year and down 30 per cent the next. That may be fine if you were invested for the ride up; it's frightening if you bought at or near the top.

The Characteristics of Bank Funds

Bank mutual funds are, as one would expect, more conservative as a group than other funds. And the banks' asset allocation models – the recommended mix of stocks, fixed income securities and cash – are also more conservative, less oriented towards stocks than the models of their brokerage firm subsidiaries. The performance of bank equity funds reflects this conservatism.

In October 1993, Duff Young, a senior analyst with the Equion Group in Toronto, evaluated the performance of Canada's largest equity funds (those that are available without any initial load or sales charge) over five periods from 1988 to the middle of 1993. The study compared each fund to all other equity funds.

One would have expected the bank funds to do well, since the largest and smallest funds tend to underperform, and the largest independents are four to five times larger than funds managed by banks or trusts. That's not what Young discovered, however. In fact, the independents' funds – Trimark Equity, Altamira Equity, Mackenzie Industrial Growth, AGF Canadian and Dynamic Fund of Canada – performed the best. The banks did worst, and the trust companies were in between.

There are several reasons for the banks' underperformance. First, they don't even try to hit home runs. They are happy to be in the second quartile. Doing a lot better usually involves greater risks than the banks are willing to take. They realize that steady performance over many years often leads to better long-term results than a 30 per cent return one year and a negative return the next. The performance of Mackenzie's Industrial Growth Fund, which took its investors from riches to rags to riches, would be unacceptable to the bank and, one presumes, to its clients.

Most of those clients are used to ultra-conservative deposit accounts, Canada Savings Bonds and GICs. They are less willing to take risks, tend to be a little less well informed, and have fewer resources than those who seek out the funds of the independents. "We want to be within the customers' range of expectations," Edgar Legzdins, vice-president of investment fund products at the Bank of Montreal, says. "If you go too high, they get nervous that you are taking on too much risk." [3]

Also, the banks have less experience with equity funds, which normally have the best performance. Their early experience was with money market and mortgage funds. Their performance in these areas, and with bond funds, is much better.

Finally, the banks don't get the best returns because they don't attract the top money managers. They are too cheap to pay them as much as independent firms are willing to pay. Industry observers believe that top performer Sue Coleman left CIBC for Altamira for just that reason, and because she was offered a stake in the firm. Independents give managers ownership and a sense of entrepreneurship that is lacking in big, bureaucratic organizations like the banks. (Royal Trust's star Paul Starita was given control of Royal Bank's $14 billion fund empire when the bank took over the trust company. He lasted less than six months, since he couldn't cope with the bank's languid decision-making process.)

While the banks are willing to hire outside managers for their international funds, they are unwilling – so far, at least – to do so for domestic funds. And since bank salaries at all levels are relatively low, it's hard within the banks to justify the sort of salaries that are required to get the top people.

The same tension exists between the banks and their brokerage subsidiaries, with the banks paying far less to their executives than their more generous, performance-oriented brokerage firms pay to theirs. In 1993, for example, Royal Bank chairman Allan Taylor raked in $1.3 million (down from $2.1 million in 1991); a number of people at subsidiary RBC Dominion Securities, which is a fraction the size of the bank, were thought to have pulled down $5 million.

Nevertheless, the banks' mutual fund performance is probably adequate for most customers. It should improve as their track record lengthens and their underperforming managers are replaced, perhaps by outsiders. The banks, however, face a more serious challenge – to deliver good service from well-informed bank personnel. This is difficult to do over such vast branch networks. As things stand, poorly informed bank customers seek guidance from poorly informed bank staff. (Remember that the banks are allowed to give advice, but not to charge for it.)

Dan Richards, president of Marketing Solutions, a Toronto-based firm that consults for the financial services industry, has surveyed the reactions of financial institutions to potential customers seeking investment advice. In a 1993 survey based on visits to 250 branches, trusts scored a failing 48 out of 100, while the banks got an even more dismal 40. Brokers and financial planners got "a good solid B" in a 1994 survey.

About 70 per cent of bank and trust company personnel didn't even ask for the name of the potential investor, or offer their own name. Only 3 per cent of bank and 6 per cent of trust staff asked for the customer's telephone number. One survey participant reported that she encountered excellent service and poor service at branches of the Royal Bank that were six blocks apart (a point that reinforces one of our themes – that it's more important to choose the right banker and branch than the right bank).[4]

As editor of the Personal Affairs section of the *Globe*'s Report on Business, I sent out a 41-year-old woman at the height of RRSP season to find out how Toronto-area financial institutions would advise her to invest $10,000. While she discovered that service was quite good, she found privacy to be a major problem.

She was forced to discuss her financial affairs at a counter in front of other people. (If this happens to you, ask if you can move to a private office.) She concluded that you should do your financial planning elsewhere – where people are better informed – and that you should "be clear about your goals. You may not have an agenda but the person you speak to will." [5]

Certainly the banks are concerned about the need to improve service. I received calls from most of the institutions mentioned in the article, asking for more details and the names of the bank personnel involved. (We used pseudonyms in the article. I refused to provide the names.)

There is a positive side to the relationship between the customer and the bank employee selling mutual funds. Unlike some financial planners and brokers, bank staff are not on commission and will not get a free trip to Hawaii for selling you a particular fund. And because most branches are so accessible, the last thing they want is an unhappy customer who they're required to deal with two or three times a week.

Tips on Buying Mutual Funds

Mutual funds are a good idea for small or novice investors, and for those without the time or interest to choose their own stocks or bonds. They are a good idea for bigger fish, too. As mentioned, they offer diversification, liquidity, professional management and, often, very good performance. Anyone who has ever bought and sold stocks and bonds for their own portfolio will know how hard it is to produce consistent returns, or to time the ups and downs of the market.

Funds can also offer discipline. Since they should always be seen as long-term investments and are ideal for RRSPs, they can be bought through a dollar-cost-averaging plan. You contribute the same amount through pre-authorized payments each month

– say $500 – so that when prices are high you buy fewer fund units, and when prices are low you buy more. It's a way to ensure you buy on a regular basis in a disciplined way, without trying to judge the market. Left to their own devices, retail investors have an uncanny ability to buy and sell at precisely the wrong moment. They buy when enthusiasm is high (as are prices) and sell when investors are discouraged and prices have troughed. They buy a Far East fund when they see that it's up 70 per cent in a year, just in time for the inevitable correction.

The first step in choosing a mutual fund is to decide what your investment goals are. Banks and brokerage firms all have asset allocation models showing what is appropriate for your age, circumstances and tolerance for risk. Normally, you should be most aggressive when you are in your twenties and least aggressive when you are retired or approaching retirement. Cash or cash equivalents (such as treasury bills) are at the low-risk end of the spectrum, and specialty equity funds (such as resource stocks) and most foreign funds are at the high-risk end (in part, because of currency risks). You also have to decide whether you need income alongside capital gains; the older you are, the more likely you are to need a steady income stream.

CIBC, typically, outlines four different "stages of life": early career, career building, asset accumulation and retirement. The recommended average savings portion (deposits, treasury bills and money market funds) over the four stages is 10 per cent; the average fixed income component (GICs and bonds) is 60 per cent; and the average stock portion is 30 per cent. By comparison, brokerage firms – with a bias towards growth – typically recommend 25 per cent more stock and 25 per cent less fixed income securities.

View your portfolio as an integrated whole. The mutual funds you buy should fit in with your other holdings. A conservative investor might even be smart to buy a high-risk resource fund if it is only 5 per cent of a well-diversified portfolio. Surprisingly, such a choice can lessen the risk of the portfolio, because resource funds are countercyclical to bonds. Inflation will make the price of bonds go down and the price of resources go up; deflation will do the opposite.

Know your goals and learn as much as you can about your investment options. Read the business press. Follow the financial markets as best you can. Read the prospectus of any mutual fund you are thinking of buying. The name of a fund and what it contains can be two different things. An analysis of 200 Canadian equity funds revealed that fewer than a quarter had more than 85 per cent of their assets in Canadian stocks.[6] Ultimately, you have to take responsibility for your investment decisions, whether they are made by you or by someone else. Ill-informed or misled investors pay a heavy price, as investors learned from the collapse of the Edmonton-based Principal Group in the late 1980s.

Knowledge about investing is improving, but is still abysmal. Dan Richards of Marketing Solutions made some horrifying discoveries when he surveyed purchasers of fixed income funds in December 1993. Asked if mutual funds invested in Canadian bonds or mortgages are insured by the Canadian government, 51 per cent of respondents said yes, 36 per cent said no and 13 per cent said they didn't know. In other words, almost two-thirds were wrong or didn't know: no mutual fund is insured by the Canadian government (though if a fund company goes under, investors are protected by the fact that the securities it holds are segregated from the company's assets). Similarly, asked about the effect of a rise in interest rates on bond or mortgage funds, only 35 per cent correctly replied that they would go down in value. Surprisingly, the more affluent investors made the most mistakes, possibly because they were inexperienced "GIC refugees" with a lot to invest.

Twelve hundred Canadians across the country responded to

Marketing Solutions' Canadian Personal Finance Literacy Test in April 1994. Respondents on average correctly answered only 38 per cent of multiple choice questions. Their lack of knowledge was quite shocking. For example, almost half the respondents couldn't pick the correct definition of a capital gain ("an increase in the value of stocks and bonds") from five choices. Even among those who owned mutual funds or stocks, one in four didn't know what a capital gain is.

What should you look for in a fund? The most obvious thing is performance, though it is only one of a number of considerations. Past performance is no guarantee of future performance, but a good track record certainly helps. Look at the record of the recent past – say one year – and at a longer period, typically five years. Compare the performance of the fund you are considering with others in the same category (comparing, say, a mortgage fund with another mortgage fund, not with an equity fund). One complication is that funds have an "end date" bias, which means that recent performance can artificially inflate or deflate earlier numbers. For example, a lot of gold funds did disastrously for years, but returned more than 100 per cent in 1993. That vastly improved their 3- and 5-year records, making it appear as though they had been doing well all along. Investors can get around this problem by looking at a fund's return for each preceding calendar year. Remember that performance can change dramatically when managers change, so make sure that the manager who produced great results for the fund is still in charge.

Look for a fund with an appropriate degree of risk. If you need only a 10 per cent return to reach your financial goals, don't buy a high-risk emerging nations fund. Mutual fund listings in the financial press usually include an assessment of risk under the term volatility. The higher the volatility, the higher the risk.

Don't become fixated on extraordinary results and expect

them to continue forever. Most fund returns ultimately revert to the mean; that is, they return from over- or underperformance to average performance. "This year's champ is next year's chump," says Robert Powell, the editor of the Boston-based *Mutual Fund Market News.* The *News* published a 1993 study which showed that investors who bought the 100 equity funds with the best 10-year records did about the same as those who bought the 100 with the worst, over a variety of periods.[7]

Stay diversified and stay realistic. A good way to do that is to know what returns you can expect, by looking at averages over many years. The average annual compound return between 1949 and 1993 was 12.9 per cent for American stocks, 10 per cent for Canadian stocks, 8 per cent for five-year GICs, 7.2 per cent for Canada Savings Bonds, 6.9 per cent for long-dated bonds and 6.3 per cent for treasury bills. Inflation averaged 4.5 per cent, which means that the real (inflation-adjusted) return on Canadian stocks was 5.5 per cent, and on bonds 2.4 per cent. If inflation remains as low as it has been recently – let's say 2 per cent – the equivalent nominal return is going to be 7.5 per cent for stocks and 4.4 per cent for bonds. In short, low inflation is almost certain to spell single-digit investment returns – so get used to them. (Obviously, these long-term returns may bear little resemblance to shorter term returns. For example, Canadian bonds outperformed stocks for the decade from 1983 to 1993, because it was a period of falling interest rates.)

Mutual fund investors should also assess the fees that funds charge. Bank and trust funds don't charge loads, so that is one sticky question out of the way. (The fierce, ongoing debate as to whether load funds perform better is becoming increasingly irrelevant, since virtually all new funds are no-load.) Check the newspaper for a fund's management expense ratio or MER, and ensure that it is in line with the competition. The MER includes all management and operating expenses and is expressed as a percentage of the fund's total net assets. Management fees (but not loads) are deducted from published performance figures (so if fees are 2 per cent and the published return is 12 per cent, the actual return was 14 per cent).

Expect fees to be the highest for international funds, followed by equity funds (typically, 2 to 2.5 per cent), bond and mortgage funds (1.5 per cent) and money market funds (0.5 to 1.5 per cent). As competition spreads beyond performance, sales commissions will be squeezed, and fees should decline.

Finally, a few general, all-weather tips:
• Canada is a dinky country with an uncertain future whose markets account for about 2 per cent of global markets. By comparison, the United States accounts for about 35 per cent and Japan slightly less. Escape our dinkyosity and take advantage of the full 20 per cent of your RRSP that can be invested in foreign securities.
• Mutual funds are a good choice for your RRSP. If you can, contribute the maximum to your plan. Once you reach the limit, put investments that receive the most favourable tax treatment – equities, equity funds and dividend funds – outside your RRSP.
• If you buy load funds, buy them through a discount broker, if you have one. Discounters have drastically reduced loads, which in any event are highly negotiable, particularly if your purchase is a large one.
• Bulls can make money, bears can make money, but pigs end up as bacon. Don't get greedy. And don't sell a fund in panic. First, mutual funds should be long-term investments. Second, sell orders for funds – unlike stocks – aren't acted upon the minute you place the order. This was a painful revelation to American investors during the stock market crash of Black Monday, October 19, 1987. It was clear the markets would be in trouble when they opened in New York on Monday morning, so many mutual fund

customers of Fidelity, the largest fund organization in North America, placed sell orders on Saturday and Sunday. Since funds are redeemed when the mutual fund company decides to process them, Fidelity's weekend sell orders went through at the end of trading on Monday, the lowest point of the crisis.

Should You Buy a Bank Fund?

There is no compelling reason to buy a bank fund. You should evaluate the fund as you would any other. Compare the bank fund you are considering with others in the same category. Is there any reason, for example, why you shouldn't buy the excellent bond and income funds offered by Altamira, instead of those offered by your bank? Probably not. Don't buy your bank's fund simply because the branch is convenient, and you picked up a brochure when you were last there.

As a group, bank funds do have disadvantages, as we have seen. Performance is often indifferent and investors who need guidance and follow-up advice will have trouble getting it. The choice of funds is growing, but is still limited. The Bank of Montreal, for example, didn't even have a regular equity fund until 1993; instead, it offered an equity index fund (which is designed to reflect the Toronto Stock Exchange 300 index). Its performance has been poor.

If you do buy a bank fund, buy it on its own merits, not because the bank will give you a break on a loan or a GIC. But if you have decided to buy a bank fund, don't hesitate to press for an advantage in some other area. Never buy all one institution's funds, whether the institution is a bank, a trust or an independent. Buying funds that belong to a variety of fund groups (which mutual fund companies love to call families) provides some diversification, beyond what is provided by holding different types of funds, and funds invested in different countries. After all, the fund managers for Dynamic Funds Management get together regularly to discuss their investment strategy, so there is bound to be overlap among their offerings.

Finally, if you have a lot of money in cash, leave as little of it in deposit accounts and as much of it in money market funds as you can. It's a painless way to pick up several percentage points on your return, and sometimes much more.

Mutual fund buyers can turn to Gordon Pape's annual *Buyer's Guide to Mutual Funds* for specific recommendations. In the 1994 edition, he ranks Royal Trust as the second-best group, after Altamira, for no-load funds. (It is unclear how much Royal Trust's funds will change, now that they have been taken over by the Royal Bank.) As for bank and trust funds, Pape recommends, as above average, Canada Trust's Everest Special Equity Fund and Everest Stock Fund; Royal Trust's American Stock Fund; CIBC-owned Hyperion Asian Trust (an aggressive fund that has a load); Montreal Trust's Excelsior's International, Dividend, Total Return and Money Market funds; CIBC's Canadian Bond Fund and its Mortgage Fund; CIBC-owned and distributed Talvest Income Fund and Talvest Money Fund; Everest Bond Fund; the Bank of Montreal's First Canadian Bond Fund and its Mortgage Fund; Green Line Canadian Bond Fund and Mortgage Fund; Royal Trust Bond Fund; RoyFund Bond Fund; Green Line Canadian Money Market Fund; Laurentian Money Market Fund; and RoyFund Money Market Fund.

Guaranteed Investment Certificates (GICs)

GICs are the Honda Accords of the investment world, reliable but dull. Cautious Canucks spend billions on them every year. According to Marketing Solutions, at the rates that prevailed in early 1994, half the GIC refugees will move back to GICs when they return 8 per cent and almost all of them at 10 per cent.

Until rates started to slide in the early 1990s, the magic figure was 10 per cent. Readers of this book will know, however, that what really counts is not the nominal interest rate but the inflation-adjusted rate.

There's nothing wrong with GICs, as long as investors are aware of the alternatives, of which there are a lot (Canada Savings Bonds, term deposits, strip bonds, mortgage-backed securities, and so on). GICs are locked-in deposits, usually for periods of one to five years, with guaranteed returns. They are covered by the Canada Deposit Insurance Corp., discussed earlier. Remember that no portion of a deposit invested for longer than five years is insured.

The single best GIC strategy is to stagger maturity dates by buying one-, two-, three-, four- and five-year GICs, so that one matures ever year. You replace the maturing GIC with a five-year certificate. The investments just keep rolling over. This strategy takes the guesswork and risk out of interest rates, because every year you lock in the prevailing rate. You renew with five-year GICs because they normally offer the highest rate.

GICs now come with an amazing array of options. The key thing to determine is the effective interest rate, which as we have seen depends upon when and how often the investment is compounded, and at what rate. It may be the original rate, or the anniversary rate. If, for example, you are interested in the Bank of Montreal's popular Escalator GIC, which offers five different rates over a five-year term, you should look past the 10 per cent rate for the fifth year, which was featured in all the ads when it was introduced, and calculate the blended rate (which was 8.08 per cent). Similarly, if you are interested in a monthly-pay GIC, ask your bank what the compounded rate over a year is, and compare it to the rate on a one-year GIC.

A number of financial institutions offer equity-linked GICs, the return on which is determined in part by the performance of the stock market. For example, the Canada Trust Blue Chip Term Deposit offers a three-year GIC with a minimum 3 per cent annual rate of return, or half the annual total return of the Toronto Stock Exchange 100 index, if that exceeds 3 per cent. So if the market gains 10 per cent, you get 5 per cent, which is probably less than a three-year GIC. You get lesser returns on both fronts – the stock market and the guaranteed portion – in exchange for protection against very weak or down years in the stock market. You are getting a hybrid product that for each of those three years could return less than a regular GIC and less than an equity fund. In my view, you are better off either with a regular GIC or an equity fund, or with splitting your money between the two – with whatever choice best fits your risk profile.

Keep track of when your GICs are coming up for renewal. If you don't tell your bank what you want to do, it will lock you in either for the same term or for the term with the lowest interest rate. There may be an exit fee if you do not renew your certificate with the same institution.

GICs are locked in, but there is a small, illiquid secondary market that trades in them. If you had the foresight to buy a "transferable" certificate, you can sell it. However, you will take a big hit on the accrued interest, and possibly even some of the principal, for the privilege of cashing it in. So do so only if you are desperately in need of money.

Like other bank products, GICs are negotiable. Your bank can probably offer you a quarter-point on interest, or even a half. Try to get a written promise that you will get a similar bonus rate if you renew your GIC with the same institution. The best opportunities arise during the spring GIC offensive (when Sunbirds return from Florida and Arizona with GICs to renew, and banks need capital to fund mortgages for the spring housing market), and during the October competition between financial institutions and the feds, with their annual Canada Savings Bond blitz.

Summary
• Mutual funds offer diversification, professional management, liquidity and often very good performance.
• Be clear about your investment goals, and stay informed.
• Maintain a diversified portfolio, which should be viewed as a unit.
• Choose funds based on performance, management and fees.
• Don't get greedy.
• Consider mutual funds to be long-term investments. Don't sell them in panic or in a crisis.
• Evaluate bank funds the way you would any other funds.
• Be aware of the effective interest rate of your GICs.
• Stagger the maturities of your GICs.

CHAPTER 8

THREATS
TO PRIVACY
AND OTHER
COMPLAINTS

How to Complain to Your Bank

If you thought there were two certainties in life – death and taxes – you're wrong. There are three. The third is this: give people the chance to complain, and they will, whether or not there is one iota of rationality to their grievance.

One caller to the federal bank regulator, the Office of the Superintendent of Financial Institutions (OSFI), said he had withdrawn more money from his account than he had intended, spent it, and wanted the bank to cough up the difference. Another had given his PIN to a friend, who had cleaned out his account; again, the bank was asked to do the decent thing and replace the funds.

These, we learn from the 1993 annual report, were two of the 12,000 complaints received by OSFI in the year ending September 1993. That's twice as many as were received in 1989, the increase being largely attributable to better public awareness about how to complain about problems with a financial institution. Many of those calls and letters were actually inquiries rather than complaints, and many dealt with non-bank concerns. "The financial institutions, we believe, are dealing effectively with their own customers," the report concludes. "We don't get very many calls or letters at all, considering the number of Canadians who have bank accounts, insurance policies, investment certifi-

205

cates, mortgages, and so on."

The banks also get complaints sent to them directly. The Bank of Montreal, for example, gets about 100 letters a month that end up at headquarters. Of course, the real number of problems will be much higher than any of these figures suggest. Some people have good reason to complain, but don't because they assume it will do no good. Others complain informally, and their complaints aren't recorded.

The top three areas of complaint to OSFI, in order, are accounts and ABMs; loans; and mortgages. There were 200 or fewer complaints about bank credit cards, and about service charges. There were even fewer about quality of service, which is what the banks themselves say their customers are most concerned about. One can surmise that on this highly personal issue, customers complain directly to the bank rather than to a third party. OSFI says it successfully mediates more than 90 per cent of the cases brought to its attention. (However, Catherine Swift, the senior vice-president of the Canadian Federation of Independent Business, says that her organization doesn't feel OSFI "is an effective advocate on the part of users of bank services. It's really, frankly, an extension of the banks and other financial institutions.")

Legislation was passed in 1992 that requires each of the banks to establish complaint procedures. They all say they are trying to "empower" the front-line troops, so that they can act on complaints themselves instead of bumping them up to a higher level. So, if you're unhappy with your financial institution, the first, most direct and fairest step is to convey your concern to the person with whom you have been dealing. If that fails, take your complaint one notch higher, which in most cases will be the branch manager. And if that fails, contact the regional head of the bank division you are dealing with.

Your last shot should be to get in touch with the president. I was amazed, while researching this book, to see how many low-level complaints make their way to the upper reaches of the banks, and how seriously the brass takes them. Smart senior bankers realize that when they deal with complaints, they generate good public relations and keep their finger on the pulse of consumer concerns and on the performance of their employees.

(Former Ford Canada president Ken Harrigan sometimes used to field calls on the company's inquiry line, answering the phone, "Customer service, Ken speaking." One irate caller demanded to speak to the president. "I am the president," replied Harrigan. "Sure. And I'm Santa Claus," the caller replied, presumably madder than ever.)

Be certain to mention at each level that if you don't get satisfaction, your next step will be to go to that person's superior and explain how the dunderheads below him or her failed to resolve the problem. This often concentrates their attention marvellously.

You can find out whom to contact at your financial institution by getting a copy of the complaints brochure at your branch or by phoning the 1-800 number all banks now have for customer information. Those numbers are also useful if you need quick information on a bank product or on current interest rates or fees. (I am less keen to use them for serious banking, though you can.) If your financial institution is provincially chartered, such as a credit union or *caisse populaire*, get in touch with your province's consumer affairs ministry.

If none of this works, write OSFI, providing full details and copies of any documents or correspondence. Always get the names of the people you are speaking to and always leave a paper trail. OSFI handles problems with banks, trusts, and loan and insurance companies. The superintendent has offices in major cities. If there isn't one listed in your phone book, contact the Office of the Superintendent of Financial Institutions, 255 Albert St., Kent Square, Ottawa, Ontario   K1A 0H2. The phone number for complaints is (613) 990-7788 and the fax is (613) 990-5591.

Don't be afraid to complain. "Consumers have to work at not being intimidated by the financial institutions that they are dealing with; they have a right to know what's going on with their money," advised OSFI's 1992 report. "One of the most frequent comments that we hear in our division is: 'I would have gone to complain at the bank, but I was afraid...'."[1]

The Problem of Privacy

I suspect that someone flipping through this book a decade from now will smirk at how naïve and quaintly old-fashioned Canadians have been about privacy and security. These two issues are rapidly moving up the public agenda. Both are being driven by advances in technology.

Consider the following example and the dilemma it creates, provided by David Livingston, TD's Visa chief.

"I could create a picture for you that says, look, you deal at Canadian Tire. We charge Canadian Tire a certain amount each time they take a credit card. I can reduce that amount, and thus reduce the amount to you – but in return, Canadian Tire would like to have information about how you spend money with them, so that they can correspond with you, to figure out how they can offer you deals, and do different things to have you spend more with them, rather than a competitor. I can charge them to have that information; I'll collect it for them.

"As a consumer, is that good for you or bad for you? How do we manage something like that? I could create a picture where that's a wonderful thing for you. I could create a picture where it's really easy that that could be abused. So to date, we don't play that game. American Express, on the other hand, have made a business out of it ...

"I think there is a thin edge there, that we're all going to have to deal with. The more information that's available, the more computers that are out there, the more we can do things that are potentially in customers' interests, but potentially not."

Canadians view privacy – the right of individuals to control the dissemination of information about themselves – as an important issue. At the same time, they see themselves as less and less able to control their own privacy. In the 1992 survey conducted for Equifax Canada by Louis Harris & Associates, more than eight out of ten Canadians said privacy of consumer information was important to them. (As a consumer issue, however, it trailed staying out of excessive debt, consumer fraud, controls over false advertising, proper labelling of the contents of food products, and environmentally safe packaging.)

Four out of five Canadians said they would consider it "extremely serious" if an unauthorized individual got access to their bank account records. Almost two out of three believed that consumers have lost all control over the way in which information about themselves is used by companies.

There is no charter or legislated guarantee of privacy for all Canadians. Quebec introduced the toughest legislation in North America with Bill 68, which prevents companies from passing information on to third parties without an individual's consent. It has already affected the approach companies are taking in other provinces.

Let's look at a specific case. The friend of a colleague at the *Globe* had had a chequing/savings account at Canada Trust for a decade.[2] The friend, a 47-year-old widow in Toronto, wrote a cheque for $44,000 to RBC Dominion Securities, which is owned by the Royal Bank, to cover the purchase of treasury bills. She was angered when she received a letter from the branch manager that began, "We at Canada Trust are most concerned when valued clients, such as you, seek other institutions for your financial needs. We are sorry to see that. We're very interested in understanding why you elected to choose one of our competitors [blah blah blah]." The manager concluded by saying that someone would follow up by phone over the next few weeks.

What right has a financial institution to single out a customer's private cheque for attention and then put the make on the customer? My response is, This is none of your business, so take a hike. It's my money, and I'll do with it what I want, whether it's donating it to Mother Theresa or blowing it at the track.

A spokeswoman for Canada Trust defended the initiative (which was perfectly legal) on the grounds that it in no way obligated the customer. The branch manager said that, after a year of sending out similar letters, the customer in question was the only one to complain.

I ran this story past a few senior bankers. One smiled and said, "That's good marketing." Another said that in the old days, when all cheques were returned to the branch, rather than stored in a data centre, banks went through all large cheques by hand. They would spot a payment of $261 to another institution at the beginning of the month, and conclude that it was payment for a loan. Large transactions are still reviewed by the bank, he said, but the information is "handled with sensitivity," whatever that means.

Another banker said he wouldn't go as far as the Canada Trust manager, but would certainly "offer services" to the customer if an investment made with a competitor came up in conversation. "We're here to help," was the line taken, which you can translate as, "We're here to grab as much business from you, and away from our competitors, as we can." Yet another banker summarized it this way. The bank, he said, wants the customer to do exactly what bank manager Mr. Drysdale wanted Jed Clampett to do in "The Beverly Hillbillies": "Don't spend that money there, Jed, keep it here."

This example of intrusiveness may sound innocuous, if annoying. But do you really want your bank to know your business? Say the banks, which have long wanted to provide "one-stop financial shopping," eventually get into the health insurance business. You're negotiating insurance with your branch, and, lo and behold, they come across the cheque you wrote for AIDS research. Do you doubt that the branch is going to have that cheque in mind when they talk to you about insurance, and about the state of your own health?

Those interested in the Bank of Montreal's financial planning program, "The Possibility Network," launched in May 1994, should keep these issues in mind when they answer the 15 personal questions, including their income and savings, on the response card.

Each of the banks has adopted a privacy code, based on a model created by the Canadian Bankers Association in 1990. Basically, it gives you the right to see and to challenge the information the bank has on you. Before the information is used for a purpose other than that for which it was collected, such as getting a loan, the bank is supposed to tell you what it is to be used for, and ask for your consent. You should be able to see a record disclosing what information about you has been made available to third parties, and to which ones.

The waiver you sign on the bottom of a loan or credit card application, usually in unreadable "mouse print," gives the credit grantor the right to see and exchange financial information about you with the credit bureau and other (unnamed) parties. The waiver on the Royal Bank's Visa application adds that if you have provided your social insurance number, the bank can use it "as an aid to identify [you] with credit bureaux and other parties." It also gives the bank the right to keep information on you even if you are no longer a client. Why should they retain that right? Well you might ask!

"We don't go to third parties," says CIBC senior vice-president Paul Vessey. "Internally, we use the information for marketing, of course we do. We're not ashamed of that either ... Do the banks sell that information, as some others do? No, we don't ... We are making better use of our cross-marketing opportunities to serve our customers better and try to broaden and deepen our relationships with them. In our view, that's the name of the game."

York University economics professor James Savary, an adviser to the Consumers' Association, worries that you may be waving your privacy rights when you sign a loan or credit card application. He has informally complained to the Canadian Bankers Association that the language used in, for example, the application for a Scotiabank Visa card violates the CBA's own privacy code.

Here's what appears – and what 99 per cent of people probably don't read – four paragraphs above the signature line on a Visa application, in smaller type than found in the attached advertising brochure. The italics are mine:

"To help maintain good relationships, Scotiabank collects information about its customers. We use this information to offer you products and services, make credit decisions, comply with the law, *protect your and our interests and for other purposes.*"

What are Scotiabank's interests? Are they likely to be your interests as well? What are "other purposes"? Couldn't they be anything the bank said they were? Where is the guarantee of privacy and the notion of meaningful consent in all this?

Finally, a story that combines a bank, a credit bureau, an unsolicited mail offer and a lot of embarrassment to the financial community. My wife received the following letter, dated October

4, 1993, from Equifax Canada. (The bold type and underlining are in the original):

"We have been asked by our customer, Citibank Canada, to help identify prospective customers in your geographical area who meet their criteria to receive a special offer. Based on this criteria, you name will be included in this select group and you may expect to hear directly from Citibank Canada in the next month or so.

Should you prefer that your name **be excluded**, please mail the return portion of this notice in the enclosed postage paid envelope before October 25, 1993."

There was a tear-off stub at the bottom of the page which read: "I **DO NOT** WISH TO BE INCLUDED IN THIS SPECIAL OFFER."

Though the letter didn't say so, the "special offer" was for a "preapproved" Visa card. Five hundred fifty-eight recipients called Equifax to complain. Most assumed (incorrectly) that Citibank had already seen their credit file. Half a dozen bankers I interviewed panned the solicitation. Neither they nor the recipients liked the "negative response" feature, which forced any recipient who didn't want the offer – and didn't want someone to gain unsolicited access to their file – to respond. The bankers also didn't like the idea of a competitor taking advantage of credit information they had submitted to the bureau, in order to increase Citibank's Visa business.

CIBC's Paul Vessey says his bank told Equifax it couldn't show CIBC's credit information to Citibank unless an application was signed that conveyed consent to see a credit file. "My fear," he explained, "is that that [offer] could risk a consumer and regulatory reaction which then will go too far the other way [on the consent question]. I think we have a good balance in this country today." Vessey said CIBC forced Equifax to "mask" his bank's data in the credit bureau's files. In May 1994, Equifax stopped providing Citibank with the data and the bank halted the program.

Even Lawrence Brown of Equifax was clearly uncomfortable when I showed him the letter, two months before the cancellation. He did, however, provide some interesting insights into how it came about. The arrangement is called "direct extraction" from Equifax's files, Brown said. Citibank gives Equifax a list of desirable postal codes and credit criteria. Equifax provides Citibank with a list of eligible names.

In Ontario, where the offer was made, the credit bureau is allowed to do this only if it informs the consumer and gives him or her the opportunity to opt out. The problem here is that "if you throw this [letter] away, you're going to get an offer," Brown said. "And you may not want that offer."

The offer is just that, an offer. Brown said Citibank still needs your consent, through a signature on the offering document, if it wants access to your credit file.

Brown said he himself had some relatives in rural areas of Ontario who were unhappy with the offer. "None of them wanted to return this, but they didn't want the offer ... That's annoying.

"I think we need to rethink the whole letter and the opt-out procedure," he concluded, after noting that this was the first time Equifax had been involved in such an initiative, and admitting the whole thing had "backfired."

What You Can Do to Protect Your Privacy

If you are concerned about privacy, always read the fine print of any agreements or waivers you sign. You're foolish not to know what you're agreeing to.

Ask whether the information your bank is asking for is required by law or is optional. On credit applications, you are entitled to leave blank the section asking for information about your spouse and the line asking for your social insurance number. Birth dates are required for retirement products. The bank is required to ask you for your SIN number before it opens an interest-bearing account. Because of concerns about money laundering, the federal government requires the banks to get information from you about cash deposits of $10,000 or more, but not large withdrawals.

Privacy is probably too nebulous an issue to complain about to the staff in the branch. Pitch your complaint higher, or contact the privacy commissioner in your province or in Ottawa (The Privacy Commissioner of Canada, 112 Kent St., Ottawa, Ontario K1A 1H3; 1-800 267-0441; fax 613 995-1501). The federal commissioner noted in his 1991-92 report that organizations such as National Defence, the RCMP and Canada Mortgage and Housing often have direct access to credit bureaus. "There appears to be potential for abuse and nothing to prevent institutions from going on fishing expeditions," the report warned. "Once in the hands of the government agency, credit information is often not kept secure."[3]

How to Get Your Name Off Unwanted Mailing and Phone Lists

If you're tired of junk mail and unwanted phone calls, there is something you can do.

Contact MPS/TPS [Mail/Telephone Preference Service], Canadian Direct Marketing Association, 1 Concorde Gate, Suite 607, Don Mills, Ontario M3C 3N6, and give them a piece of your mind (as well as your name, address, and phone number). The association, a self-regulating body that represents over 80 per cent of the direct marketing industry – including the banks – offers consumers a variety of rights, including the right to have their name removed from marketing lists, and the right to register with "Do Not Mail" and "Do Not Call" services. While you're at it, ask for a copy of their privacy code.

Should You Wave Sayonara to Privacy?

Of course, all this complaining and letter writing could be for naught, in which case your time would be better spent squeezing limes into gin and tonics. I asked former finance committee chairman Don Blenkarn whether he was worried about the privacy issue. He gave the following emphatic answer:

"Nope. I think anybody who wants to be worried about privacy is living in another age. Once we have developed the sophistication of computers, nobody's got anything private, anywhere. Forget it. If you think for one moment that your financial affairs are private.... Every bank's got you on computer. The government's got you on computer. The hospital's got you on computer. The doctor's got you on computer. Your lawyer's got you on computer. And computers talk to one another. I mean, it's gone."

Still, progress is possible. We've seen that Citibank was forced by a barrage of criticism to withdraw its "negative response," pre-approved credit card offer. And in the spring of 1993, *The Globe and Mail* prominently ran a story revealing that the Royal Bank of Canada was including client bank card numbers, which include information on where you live, in what it supplied to the market research firms it hires to test demand for products and services.[4] The card numbers were included alongside other personal data including name, address, telephone number, age and sex. A bank spokeswoman mounted an elaborate defence of the activity, despite the threat to privacy and security that it appeared to pose. The Consumers' Association termed the practice "frightening."

When the story broke, customers phoned to express their concern. The result? The Royal Bank, the country's largest financial institution, succumbed and ended the practice the same day. A senior bank official explained, "Our feeling is that if there is one more piece of information we can keep confidential, then we absolutely should and must." If that's really what the bank thought, why did it reveal the information to outsiders in the first place, and then defend the practice so vigorously?

Privacy could soon surpass the environment as a social concern. It's an even more difficult issue, and it's in many ways more insidious. Everyone can see and understand the harm that an oil slick can do to an attractive beach and to wildlife. Few, however, can anticipate or detect the potential damage of widespread or irresponsible dissemination of financial information.

More and more financial and other information is available on databases and sold to market products. It's this combination of technology and potential for profit and cross-selling that ensures that privacy can – and will – be endangered. That's why it will increasingly be a concern to Canadians, as we rush headlong towards the 21st century.

NOTES

INTRODUCTION

[1] Robert A. Bennett, "The Lessons of Canadian Banking," *United States Banker*, December 1993, p. 28.

[2] Quoted in *The Globe and Mail*, January 22, 1993.

[3] Minutes of proceedings, Industry Committee, March 22, 1994, No. 5, p. 9.

CHAPTER ONE   PERSONAL CREDIT: HOW TO GET IT AND LOSE IT

[1] Edward M. Lewis, *An Introduction to Credit Scoring* (San Rafael, Calif.: The Athena Press, 1992), p. 14.

[2] Lewis, p. 94.

CHAPTER TWO   PERSONAL LOANS

[1] *Wall Street Journal*, December 21, 1993; February 23, 1994.

[2] *The Globe and Mail*, June 29, 1993.

CHAPTER THREE   PLASTIC EXPLOSIVES AND HOW TO HANDLE THEM

[1] Standing Committee on Consumer and Corporate Affairs. McNally, November 6, 1991, No. 20, p. 54; Kelman, November 2, No. 30, p. 19; David Simpson, November 20, No. 23, p. 9.

[2] Ann Finlayson and Sandra Martin, *Card Tricks* (Toronto: Viking, 1993), p. 57.

[3] *Financial Times*, January 30, 1989, p. 25.

[4] Lawrence M. Ausubel, "The failure of competition in the credit card market," *American Economic Review*, March 1991.

[5] Minutes of proceedings, Nov. 6, 1991, No. 20, p. 46.

[6] Minutes, No. 20, p. 33, No. 20, p. 35.

7 *The Globe and Mail,* June 7, 1989.

8 *The Globe and Mail,* June 18, 1993.

9 *The Wall Street Journal,* May 3, 1993.

10 *Canadian Banker,* January/February 1992, p. 35; Canadian Association of Chiefs of Police, 1993 Organized Crime Committee Report, pp. 81-85.

CHAPTER FOUR **HOW TO GET A SMALL BUSINESS LOAN**

1 Minutes of Proceedings, House of Commons Industry Committee, No. 9, pp. 32, 43.

2 Larry Wynant and James Hatch, *Banks and Small Business Borrowers* (London: The Western Business School, the University of Western Ontario, 1990), p. 205; M.J. Grant & Co. Ltd., *Small Business Views the Banks* (Toronto: Canadian Federation of Independent Business, 1988), p. 51.

3 Wynant and Hatch, *Banks,* pp. 239-40.

4 Minutes, Industry Committee, March 22, 1994, No. 5, p. 9; April 14, No. 8, pp. 56-57.

5 Small Business Finance Conference, sponsored by the CBA, November 8, 1993.

6 Grant, *Small Business,* p. 33.

7 Jacques Vien, John Cole, February 23, House of Commons Legislative Committee on Bill C-99, No. 2, p. 11.

8 *The Globe and Mail,* August 31, 1993.

9 Ronald Rogers, senior executive vice-president, personal and commercial banking, February 23, 1993, Legislative Committee on Bill C-99, No. 2, p. 23.

10 Wynant and Hatch, *Banks,* pp. 289-94.

11 *The Globe and Mail,* November 17, 1992.

12 Barbara Orser, Allan Riding, Catherine Swift, "Banking Experiences of Canadian Micro-Businesses," *Journal of Enterprise Culture* (Singapore: World Scientific Publishing Co., 1993), Vol. I, No. 2, p. 9; Wynant and Hatch, *Banks,* p. 343.

CHAPTER FIVE **HOW TO PAY THOUSANDS LESS FOR YOUR MORTGAGE**

1 *The Globe and Mail,* June 5, 1993.

2 Morgij2 is considered the best program, though it's fairly advanced.

It's available only for IBM for $95 (plus PST for Ontario residents) from Different Products Ltd., 789 Kingsway Dr., Burlington, Ontario L7T 3H7.

[3] Ted Jackson, *Financial Times of Canada*, January 16 and February 13, 1993.

[4] *The Globe and Mail*, November 26, 1991.

CHAPTER SIX   **BANK FEES AND ACCOUNTS**

[1] This and the following testimony can be found in the proceedings of the Standing Committee on Finance and Economic Affairs, April 12-21, 1988.

[2] J.L. Carr, G.F. Mathewson, N.C. Quigley, *Ensuring Failure* (Toronto: C.D. Howe Institute, 1994), vii, viii, 52.

CHAPTER SEVEN   **MUTUAL FUNDS AND GICS**

[1] *The Globe and Mail*, August 19, 1993.

[2] Patrick McKeough, *Investor's Digest*, December 10, 1993 and February 18, 1994; see also the *Canadian Mutual Fund Adviser*, June 14, 1994; Douglas Goold, Market Watch, *The Globe and Mail*, September 22, 1993.

[3] *Toronto Star*, October 21, 1993.

[4] Marketing Solutions, "Asking for Advice: What happens when customers go to financial institutions for investment advice" (Toronto, 1993). *The Financial Post*, January 20, 1994; *The Globe and Mail*, May 29, 1993.

[5] Helen Kohl Clayton, "Sorting through RRSP sales pitches," *The Globe and Mail*, Feb. 20, 1993.

[6] *Canadian Investment Review*, Vol. VII, No. 1 (spring 1994), p. 5; Douglas Goold, Market Watch, *The Globe and Mail*, July 13, 1994.

[7] Douglas Goold, "Be responsible: use a dart board," Market Watch, *The Globe and Mail*, March 7, 1994.

CHAPTER EIGHT   **THREATS TO PRIVACY AND OTHER COMPLAINTS**

[1] OSFI, 1992 Report, p. 3.

[2] Ellen Roseman, *The Globe and Mail*, March 24, 1993.

[3] Annual Report, 1991-92, Privacy Commissioner, pp. 77-78.

[4] *The Globe and Mail*, March 8-9, 1993.

GLOSSARY

Affinity card: A credit card that has a promotional arrangement with an affiliated organization, such as a university or a charity. They are more common in the United States than in Canada.

Amortization: The number of years it will take to repay a mortgage in full, and hence the length of time used to calculate regular payments.

Automated banking machine (ABM): Also called automated teller machine or ATM. A terminal where a customer can perform banking tasks, such as making deposits and paying bills. The use of the machine is normally free for the bank's customers, but costs $1 a time for users from other banks.

Bank Act: The federal legislation governing the banks. It is normally updated every 10 years.

Bank card: A card issued by a financial institution that identifies the holder as that institution's customer. It is used for ABM transactions. "Bank card" can also refer to a bank's debit card or credit card.

Bank of Canada: Canada's central bank, with headquarters on Bank Street in Ottawa. The Federal Reserve Bank is its equivalent in the United States; central banks abroad include the Bank of England and the Bundesbank. The Bank of Canada's governor and board are responsible for this country's monetary policy, that is, for preserving the value and integrity of the currency, normally by maintaining price stability (in other words, by controlling inflation).

Basis point: One one-hundredths of a percentage point. If a 6.25 per cent lending rate is increased by 15 basis points, the new rate is 6.40 per cent.

Caisse populaire: A credit union operating in Quebec or in another French-speaking area of Canada. Each is cooperatively owned by its members and provincially regulated.

Canada Deposit Insurance Corporation (CDIC): A Crown corporation that insures certain deposits, normally to a maximum of $60,000 per depositor for each member financial institution, against the failure of that institution.

Charge cards: Cards, such as most of those issued by American Express, that require payment in full each month.

Chartered banks: Banks that are governed by the Bank Act. They are called either Schedule I (which includes the Big Six banks; no single shareholder of a Schedule I bank is allowed to hold more than a 10 per cent voting stake) or Schedule II (most of which are foreign banks operating in Canada, and do not have this ownership restriction).

Closed and open mortgages: A closed mortgage cannot be paid off before maturity, except with the lender's permission and the payment of a penalty. Mortgages can be partially open or fully open. A fully open mortgage can be prepaid any time before the mortgage comes due, without penalty or notice.

Collateral: Security pledged by a borrower to a creditor, who can sell the collateral if the loan is not repaid.

Consumer credit: A form of commerce by which an individual obtains money, goods or services in return for a promise to repay, along with an interest charge, at some specified future date.

Credit cards: Credit cards, such as Visa and MasterCard, offer revolving credit, so that balances can be carried from statement to statement as long as minimum payments (usually 5 per cent of the outstanding balance) are made.

Credit rating: An assessment of an individual's (or a company's) credit history and ability to repay obligations.

Creditworthiness: Creditworthiness is an individual's (or institution's) suitability for credit. It is determined by assessing risk.

Credit unions: Provincially regulated financial service cooperatives, which are owned and controlled by their members. While there are provincial and national credit union organizations, each credit union operates independently.

Debit card: A card that allows the cost of a purchase to be automatically deducted – for a transaction fee – from a holder's bank account.

Effective interest rate: The rate you pay after the effects of compounding are taken into account. The more frequently a rate is compounded (or calculated), the higher the effective rate. The nominal rate, by comparison, is the rate that is quoted or posted and does not take compounding into account.

Fixed rate and variable rate mortgages: A fixed rate mortgage has an interest rate that remains the same for the term of the mortgage. A variable (or floating) rate mortgage has a rate that is set by the lender every month. It is usually based on the prime rate offered by the institution.

Grace period: The period between the statement date and the due date on a card.

Guaranteed Investment Certificate (GIC): A certificate issued by a financial institution confirming an interest-bearing deposit with a fixed return and fixed maturity (normally from one to five years).

High-ratio mortgage: A mortgage that exceeds 75 per cent of the lesser of the appraised value of a property, or its purchase price. By law, it must be insured by the Canada Mortgage and Housing

Corporation, a Crown corporation.

Line of credit: An agreement between a lender and a borrower establishing a maximum amount upon which the borrower may draw, whenever he or she sees fit. Normally a minimum of 3 to 5 per cent is repayable each month.

Mortgage: Usually a loan to pay for the purchase of a property, which becomes the collateral or security for that loan.

Mortgage term: The length of time covered by a mortgage agreement. Most terms in Canada range from six months to five years. The term is normally shorter than the amortization period.

Mutual fund: A professionally managed investment pool. Most funds are open-ended, issuing and redeeming shares or units on an ongoing basis. A few are closed-end funds, which have a fixed number of shares, and can be traded – just like stocks – on stock exchanges.

Office of the Superintendent of Financial Institutions: Ottawa-based OSFI regulates all federally incorporated financial institutions, including banks.

Prime rate: The interest rate that financial institutions charge their most creditworthy customers, most of whom are large corporations, for short-term loans. Other lending rates are based on it.

Real return: The return you earn after inflation is taken into account. For example, if you earn 10 per cent interest in a year that inflation is 4 per cent, your real return is 6 per cent.

Refinance: To refinance a loan or mortgage is to pay it in full, and arrange for a new loan or mortgage with the same or a different lender.

Registered retirement savings plans (RRSPs): Federal government-sponsored plans that allow a holder to save for his or her retirement without paying tax on the capital gains and interest earned on investments in the plan.

Small business: A business that employs fewer than 50 full-time employees and has gross annual sales of less than $5 million.

Spread: The difference between the interest rate paid to depositors and the rate charged to borrowers.

Trust company: A federally or provincially regulated financial institution that offers essentially the same services as the banks. Trusts can be less widely held (Canada Trust, for example, is 98 per cent controlled by Imasco Ltd.). Unlike the banks, trusts don't have access to the Bank of Canada as a lender of last resort. Trust company deposits are protected by the Canada Deposit Insurance Corp.

FURTHER READING

Cohen, Bruce. *The Money Adviser: The Canadian Guide to Successful Financial Planning.* Toronto: Stoddart, 1994.

Finlayson, Ann and Martin, Sandra. *Card Tricks: Bankers, Boomers and the Explosion of Plastic Credit.* Toronto: Penguin, 1993. (An expanded paperback edition will be published in the fall of 1994.)

Gray, Douglas A. *Home Buying Made Easy: The Canadian Guide to Purchasing a Newly Built or Pre-Owned Home.* Whitby, Ont.: McGraw-Hill Ryerson, 1993.

Gray, Douglas A. *Mortgages Made Easy: The Canadian Guide to Home Financing.* Whitby: McGraw-Hill, 1993.

Kelman, Steven G. *Understanding Mutual Funds: Your No-Nonsense Everyday Guide.* Toronto: Penguin, 1994.

Pape, Gordon. *1994 Buyer's Guide to Mutual Funds.* Scarborough, Ont.: Prentice-Hall Canada, 1993.

Silverstein, Alan. *The Perfect Mortgage: Your Key to Cutting the Cost of Home Ownership.* Toronto: Stoddart, 1993.

Vaz-Oxlade, Gail. *The Borrower's Answer Book.* Toronto: Stoddart, 1993.

INDEX